Strategies & Tactics for the MPRE

for the **MPRE**

Multistate Professional Responsibility Exam

This edition by
Lazar Emanuel
J.D., Harvard Law School

Prior editions by
Kimm Alayne Walton, J.D.

ASPEN

PUBLISHERS

1185 Avenue of the Americas, New York NY 10036
www.aspenpublishers.com

© 2005 Aspen Publishers, Inc.
A WoltersKluwer Company
www.aspenpublishers.com

Permissions
Aspen Publishers
1185 Avenue of the Americas
New York, NY 10036

Printed in the United States of America

ISBN 0-7355-5166-9

This book is intended as a general review of a legal subject. It is not intended as a source of advice for the solution of legal matters or problems. For advice on legal matters, the reader should consult an attorney.

About Aspen Publishers

Aspen Publishers, headquartered in New York City, is a leading information provider for attorneys, business professionals, and law students. Written by preeminent authorities, our products consist of analytical and practical information covering both U.S. and international topics. We publish in the full range of formats, including updated manuals, books, periodicals, CDs, and online products.

Our proprietary content is complemented by 2,500 legal databases, containing over 11 million documents, available through our Loislaw division. Aspen Publishers also offers a wide range of topical legal and business databases linked to Loislaw's primary material. Our mission is to provide accurate, timely, and authoritative content in easily accessible formats, supported by unmatched customer care.

To order any Aspen Publishers title, go to *www.aspenpublishers.com* or call 1-800-638-8437.

To reinstate your manual update service, call: 1-800-638-8437.

For more information on Loislaw products, go to *www.loislaw.com* or call 1-800-364-2512.

For *Customer Care issues, e-mail CustomerCare@aspenpublihsers.com*; call 1-800-234-1660; or fax 1-800-901-9075.

Aspen Publishers
A Wolters Kluwer Company

This book is dedicated to the thousands of lawyers who will follow me in the noble profession of the law. My hope is that my work will help them to enter the profession.

Table of Contents

Part One
Plan of Attack for the MPRE

A. Introduction

The Multistate Professional Responsibility Examination (MPRE) is a hurdle you can't dodge if you want to practice law anywhere in the United States. The exam is designed to test your knowledge of two relatively short documents, the ABA Model Rules of Professional Conduct and the ABA Code of Judicial Conduct, as well as your "understanding of the generally accepted rules, principles and common law regulating the legal profession in the United States."

The exam consists of 50 multiple-choice questions, each calling for one correct answer among four options. The passing grade is different from state to state, but it is generally in the range of 70–80. To find the passing grade for your state, contact the state board of bar examiners.

By the time you finish your law school course in ethics or professional responsibility, you will have developed a general sense of the range of ethical problems lawyers face every working day. All you have to do to get past the MPRE is to apply this general sense to specific fact patterns created by the MPRE examiners.

Problems in legal ethics do not lend themselves easily to multiple choice questions. They are more logically dealt with in the essay format which permits extensive discussion of alternatives and the statement of a nuanced conclusion. Believe it or not, this actually makes the MPRE a lot easier than most tests. There's a good reason for this—in order for a multiple choice exam to be valid, the answers have to be *unquestionably* correct. The kiss of death for a multiple choice question is to lead you to conclude "Well, the answer is A if you interpret it this way, and B if you interpret it this other way."

This simple fact—that each MPRE question has to have one, indisputably correct answer—means that the questions and answers have to be written with especially broad strokes. In fact, MPRE questions and answers are written with such broad strokes that in a lot of cases you will be able to pick out the right answer at first glance. We'll show you how to do this a little later in this section. Our point right now is only this — the MPRE isn't particularly difficult, and with the advice in this book and a little extra preparation, you should pass it quite easily.

That doesn't mean you can wander into the exam room on test day and hope for the best. But it does mean that you'll have a less hectic time studying for it than you would for most exams. Frankly, there are only two things that you really need to do: one is to get familiar with the ethics rules, and the other is to get a sense of the kinds of questions that appear on the MPRE.

In learning the ethics rules, your primary sources will be the Model Rules of Professional Conduct and the Code of Judicial Conduct. The MPRE also tests a number of areas that you won't learn from the two Codes, like the whole area of legal malpractice.

As you know by now, the ABA Codes are incredibly tedious to read. (After all, they were written by lawyers for lawyers.) So you'd be well advised to expand your preparation into a few more tools than the Codes themselves. We recommend especially the *Law in a Flash* cards on Professional Responsibility, which you will find at just about any law school bookstore. The flashcards offer more than 900 cards testing every aspect of both Codes. They define the basic rules and then give you hundreds of hypothetical fact patterns just like the ones tested on the MPRE. They have been revised and updated to reflect the most recent changes in the Model Rules of Professional Conduct and the Code of Judicial Conduct. The cards take only about 8–10 hours to review. They incorporate modern learning techniques that not only teach you the rules, but also how to apply those rules to facts quickly and effectively.

Of course, you can use any source to review the ethics rules, such as outlines or hornbooks. The point is, you have to know the rules. Other than that, you have to learn the structure and technique of MPRE questions. And that's what this book will show you. In Part One, we'll show you how to attack MPRE questions, and in Part Two, we'll give you a chance to put this plan of attack into practice on some model MPRE Questions and Answers. In Part Three, you're completely on your own — we've reproduced sample National Conference of Bar Examiners (NCBE) questions and the corresponding answer key. See if you can pick the right answer. Be careful! We know you'll be tempted to skip this first part and plunge right into the practice questions. We recommend strongly against that. If you have only a few hours to prepare for the MPRE, use them to read and understand Part One of this book. If you put our plan of attack to work for you, you won't fail the MPRE unless you want to.

There are only 50 practice questions in this book. If you were expect-
ing to review thousands of questions for the MPRE — relax. The reason there are only 50 review questions is that they do the whole job of
teaching you how to deal with the exam. With the plan of attack we'll
lay out for you and these 50 review questions, you have virtually all
the tools you need. You'd be better off spending the rest of your
study time doing substantive review of the Codes themselves. (If you
feel the need for more, spend a few hours on the *Law in a Flash*
flashcards.) You shouldn't need any other tools.

Incidentally, all of the questions in this book — the ones we use for
examples in Part One, the model questions in Part Two and the practice questions in Part Three — are real MPRE questions. They've all
appeared on actual MPREs in prior years, and they're in this book
courtesy of the NCBE. So you don't have to worry that the questions
in this book may not resemble the ones you'll see on your MPRE; they
were written by the very same people who'll write your MPRE!

B. Basic Information About the MPRE

Background — The MPRE is created and administered by the NCBE,
which is also responsible for the Multistate Bar Examination. The
MPRE is currently administered in virtually every state, as well as the
District of Columbia.

When Offered — The MPRE is administered three times a year — in
March, August, and November. In many states, you can take the
MPRE before you finish law school; most students who do so take
the exam in March of their final year of law school.

Format and Length — The MPRE is a 50-question, multiple choice
exam which lasts approximately three hours (beginning and ending
times vary depending on the size of the testing center and the number
of rooms available). It is similar to the Multistate Bar Examination in
the sense that each question includes a fact pattern followed by four
answer choices, from which you are supposed to choose the "best"
response. Later in Part One we'll give you lots of examples of
this question format, and you'll learn to analyze it down to its most
essential elements.

Coverage — The MPRE now covers the ABA Model Rules of Professional Conduct as currently amended, as well as the ABA Code of
Judicial Conduct. It doesn't attempt to cover the code of any individual

state. (In actual practice you may find that the codes governing professional responsibility in your state differ in substantial respects from the ABA Codes.)

As the 2002 MPRE Sample Questions VI booklet published by the NCBE informs us, the MPRE also tests the applicant's "understanding of the generally accepted rules, principles and common law regulating the legal profession...; in these items, the correct answer will be governed by the view reflected in the majority of cases, statutes, or regulations on the subject." In testing issues such as litigation sanctions or the attorney-client evidentiary privilege, the Federal Rules of Civil Procedure and the Federal Rules of Evidence apply.

The entire subject of legal malpractice, which is of vital concern to lawyers and which is tested on the MPRE, is not mentioned as such in the Model Rules.

Scoring — Your MPRE score is determined by how many questions you answer correctly; there's no penalty for incorrect answers. The lesson to be learned from this is that it pays to answer every question, even if you're not exactly sure what the correct answer is.

How to Apply for the MPRE — To apply for the MPRE, write or call:

> National Conference of Bar Examiners
> c/o ACT, Inc.
> MPRE Application Department
> Post Office Box 4001
> 301 ACT Dr.
> Iowa City, Iowa 52243-4001

C. What the MPRE Tests

Scope of Questions

Questions on the ABA Model Rules and related sources dealing with the conduct of lawyers and law firms make up between 90-94% of all the questions on the MPRE. The remaining questions test the applicant's knowledge of the Code of Judicial Conduct.

The outline of subjects published by the NCBE lists the items tested. Occasionally, other items are added, but the NCBE's outline is a good guide to the weight you should give each subject as you study. Not all of the items are tested each time, but if you've covered them all in your studies, you can't miss.

The NCBE's outline of MPRE subjects, and the approximate weight given to each, follows:

I. Regulation of the Legal Profession (8–12%)

    A. Inherent Powers of Courts to Regulate Lawyers

    B. Admission to the Profession

    C. Regulation after Admission

    D. Maintaining Professional Standards — Peer Responsibility

    E. Unauthorized Practice

    F. Fee Division with a Non-Lawyer

    G. The Law Firm

    H. Contractual Restrictions on Practice

II. The Client-Lawyer Relationship (10–14%)

    A. Acceptance or Rejection of Clients

    B. Scope, Objective, and Means of the Representation

    C. Within the Bounds of the Law

    D. Withdrawal

    E. Client-Lawyer Contracts

    F. Fees

III. Privilege and Confidentiality — Clients and Former Clients (6–10%)

    A. Evidentiary Privilege

    B. Professional Obligation of Confidence

    C. Client-Authorized Disclosure

    D. Permissible Disclosure

    E. Special Problems

IV. Independent Professional Judgment — Conflicts of Interest — Client Consent (12–16%)

    A. As Affected by Lawyer's Personal Interest

    B. Lawyer as Witness

    C. Acquiring an Interest in Litigation

    D. Entering into Business Transactions with Client

    E. Conflicting Interests — Current Clients and Former Clients

F. Influence by Persons Other than Client

G. Law Firm, Associates, and Related Persons

H. Lawyer's Service as Arbitrator, Mediator, or Judge

V. Competence, Legal Malpractice, and Other Civil Liability (8–12%)

A. Civil Liability, Including Malpractice

B. Maintaining Competence

C. Acceptance of Employment

D. Exercise of Diligence and Care

E. Limiting Liability for Malpractice

VI. Litigation and Other Forms of Advocacy (12–16%)

A. Exercise of Professional Judgment

B. Civility, Courtesy, and Decorum

C. Conduct in the Course of Litigation — Claims, Defenses, Testimony, and Evidence

D. Fraud or Perjury

E. Communications in Course of Representation

VII. Different Roles of the Lawyer (4–8%)

A. Lawyer as Advisor

B. Lawyer as Intermediary

C. Lawyer as Evaluator

D. Lawyer as Negotiator

E. Lawyer as Mediator

F. Special Obligations of the Lawyer in Public Service

G. Appearances before Legislative Bodies

VIII. Safekeeping Property and Funds of Clients and Others (4–8%)

A. Lawyer as Trustee of Client Funds

B. Lawyer as Custodian of Client Property

C. Disputed Claims

IX. Communication About Legal Services (6–10%)

A. Public Communications About Services

B. Referrals

C. Group Legal Services

D. Direct Contact with Prospective Clients (Solicitation)

E. Fields of Practice — Limitations of Practice and Specialization

X. Lawyers and the Legal System (2–6%)

A. Lawyer Activity in Improving the Legal System

B. Impropriety Incident to Public System

XI. Judicial Ethics (6–10%)

A. Uphold the Integrity and Independence of the Judiciary

B. Avoid Impropriety and the Appearance of Impropriety

C. Duties of Impartiality and Diligence

D. Activities to Improve the Legal System

E. Extra-Judicial Activities

F. Political Activity of Judges

G. Candidate for Judicial Office

D. Attacking the MPRE

1. Getting Familiar with the Question Format

MPRE questions are arranged in this way: They start with a fact pattern set around a common problem in legal ethics. This is followed by a specific inquiry which should lead you to the right answer. This is the "call" of the question. Finally, there are four answer choices. You are expected to choose the one which best answers the call. Here's a typical example:

Attorney represented Buyer in a real estate transaction. Due to Attorney's negligence in drafting the purchase agreement, Buyer was required to pay for a survey that should have been paid by Seller, the other party to the transaction. Attorney fully disclosed this negligence to Buyer, and Buyer suggested that he would be satisfied if Attorney simply reimbursed Buyer for the entire cost of the survey.

Although Buyer might have recovered additional damages if a malpractice action were filed, Attorney reasonably believed that the proposed settlement was fair to Buyer. Accordingly, in order to forestall a malpractice action. Attorney readily agreed to make the reimbursement. Attorney drafted a settlement agreement, and it was executed by both Attorney and Buyer.

Was Attorney's conduct <u>proper</u>?

A. Yes, if Attorney advised Buyer in writing that Buyer should seek independent representation before deciding to enter into the settlement agreement.

B. Yes, because Attorney reasonably believed that the proposed settlement was fair to Buyer.

C. No, because Attorney settled a case involving liability for malpractice while the matter was still ongoing.

D. No, unless Buyer was separately represented in negotiating and finalizing the settlement agreement.

In this question, the first and second paragraphs make up the fact pattern. The final sentence, "Was Attorney's conduct proper?..." is the "call" of the question—it tells you specifically what to look for in the answer options. A through D are "answer options." One of these is the best response, and the other three are "distractors." (Incidentally, the best response is A.)

While the question design above is the the most common on the MPRE, there is a one variation that you also are likely to see on your exam. It looks like this:

Client, a new client of Attorney, has asked Attorney to write a letter recommending Client's nephew for admission to the bar. Client has told Attorney that he has no direct contact with nephew, but that Client's sister (nephew's mother) has assured Client that the nephew is industrious and honest.

Which of the following is (are) proper for Attorney?

I. Write the letter on the basis of Client's assurance.

II. Write the letter on the basis of Client's assurance if Attorney has no unfavorable information about the nephew.

III. Make an independent investigation and write the letter only if Attorney is thereafter satisfied that the nephew is qualified.

A. III only

B. I and II, but not III

C. I and III, but not II

D. I, II, and III

As you can see, the difference here is that the options you have to analyze are really I, II and III, instead of A, B, C, and D. Once you've selected the correct option(s), the answer is inevitable. The analysis you have to make is the same as in the traditional format. (Incidentally, the best response is A.)

2. Reading the Fact Patterns

On the MPRE, you have approximately three minutes to read each question, answer it, and move on. This means not only that you have to have a ready grasp of the ethics rules, but that you also must be able to read and respond quickly. Most of all, you need to know what to look for. That's what we'll discuss here.

The most important thing to keep in mind about the MPRE is that it's very limited in the range of questions that it can raise. We mentioned this point earlier, but we want to flesh it out here because it will go a long way toward "defanging" the MPRE for you.

As with all standardized multiple-choice tests, the MPRE simply cannot test gray areas; the facts must clearly point toward one and only one correct answer in order for the question to be "psychometrically" sound—i.e., in order for the question to be a valid measure of competence. In other words, there can't be a reasonable argument about which is the right answer. What this means in practical terms is best shown by example.

Let's say that you and your best friend study for the MPRE together, and you both have an equally detailed knowledge of the rules of ethics; in fact, your knowledge of the rules is identical. In order for any given question on the MPRE to be valid as a testing device, you would both have to choose the same answer. If you *didn't*, the question cannot be said to have tested your knowledge. Because you both had the same knowledge of the rules, the facts and the questions should have led you to the same result. If you each answered differently and if this one question were the difference between passing and failing the MPRE, one of you would pass and the other would fail, *even though your knowledge of the rules was identical.* From a tester's point of view, this would make the test invalid, because the test would fail its own purpose of distinguishing among students on the basis of their knowledge.

For instance, say a question involves a lawyer's representation of multiple parties who may have a conflict of interest. The issue is: can the lawyer represent all of them in light of this potential conflict. Clearly, before a lawyer can properly ask the consent of the parties to a multiple representation, he must *reasonably believe* he can represent all the parties adequately. "Reasonableness" is a standard which is totally fact-dependent. Therefore, if the Bar Examiner wanted to test you on whether the lawyer *could* properly represent all the parties in this basic circumstance, he would have to choose either of the following options:

1. Make it unmistakably clear in the facts that the lawyer's belief was reasonable; or

2. Condition the propriety of the representation on facts raising the issue of reasonableness — for instance, by saying, "The representation is proper *if* the lawyer reasonably believes he can adequately represent the parties and he obtains their fully informed consent." [We'll cover conditional answers (*"if"* answers) later.]

If the examiner failed to use either of these options, the question would not be a valid test of the rule requiring the consent in advance of all parties to a multiple-party representation. In fact, if a question that is offered on the MPRE doesn't "perform as intended" — a euphemistic term describing an ambiguous question that sneaks by the drafting committee — it's dropped from the exam.

If this theory for testing the validity of a test question isn't all that clear to you now, don't worry. The only thing that really matters is that you appreciate its impact on what you should look for in MPRE fact patterns. Let's look at some of these things individually.

a. Pay special attention to statements about the lawyer's or the client's state of mind

In many ethics rules, the propriety of a lawyer's conduct depends on whether he *knows* or *believes* something. His knowledge or belief will determine whether some act on his part is mandated or prohibited. Pay special attention to words or phrases like "knows," "knowingly," "concludes," "becomes convinced," "believes," and "reasonably believes." In fact, on many ethical issues, the attorney's belief about a fact or an event is more important than the fact or event itself.

Take a typical question about a lawyer's role in recommending a candidate for admission to the bar. A lawyer cannot "*knowingly* make a false statement of material fact*" in connection with an applicant's admission to the bar. Model Rule 8.1.

It doesn't matter whether the person you recommend later turns out to be a pimp or a drug dealer; as long as *you didn't know the true facts*, you won't be disciplined if the Bar Examiners later discover them.

Take another example — the problem of conflicts of interest. In most conflict cases, the conflict can be remedied by obtaining the informed consent of the affected clients whether they are prospective, current, or former. However, before the lawyer can even *seek* a client's consent, he must *reasonably believe* he can carry on the representation of that client without adverse affect on his representation of another client. Model Rule 1.7. Here again, it doesn't really matter whether his belief ultimately proves to be sound; as long as he *reasonably believed* at the time that he could undertake the representation without adversely affecting either party, he will not be disciplined.

We could go on and on with examples, but you get the idea; it's important to pay attention to the examiner's description of the attorney's state of mind — i.e., his beliefs and knowledge — in determining whether or not he's acted ethically.

b. Pay attention to the lawyer's motivation when she acts or fails to act

Just as the extent of an attorney's knowledge can determine the propriety or impropriety of her behavior, so too can her reasons for undertaking, or failing to undertake, the behavior. You should always make special note of the reason for an attorney's actions. Often, that will help you in assessing the propriety of her conduct.

For example, on a question dealing with permissive or mandatory withdrawal from representation, the attorney's reasons for withdrawing will be crucial in determining whether or not the withdrawal is ethical. Some questions will raise obvious issues of motivation, but others will insert more insidious circumstances in which motivation may play a less obvious but equally critical role.

Take, for instance, whether to call a particular witness at trial. Ordinarily, whether or not to call a particular witness is the exclusive decision of the attorney, not the client. Under ordinary circumstances, the attorney has acted perfectly properly if she decides *not* to call a particular witness after careful deliberation.

But suppose she decides not to call a particular witness because
it would take too much time and energy on her part to find
and prepare her. Then her motives would raise issues both of
incompetent representation under Model Rule 1.1 and of a lack
of reasonable diligence under Model Rule 1.3. When the lawyer's
behavior raises questions about her *motivation,* you have to
analyze that motivation carefully to determine whether the
behavior itself was proper.

c. Ignore "window dressing" — pay attention to the lawyer's core behavior

In some MPRE questions, the Bar Examiners test your knowledge of the ethical rules by surrounding unethical behavior with
the "trappings" of propriety. This is to test whether you can tell
the trees from the forest — i.e., to see if you can find evidence
of unethical conduct when it's surrounded by misleading
"goodies."

Let's take competence, for example. You know, of course, that
lawyers have a duty to provide competent service to their clients. A question that asked only, "Is a lawyer subject to discipline for providing incompetent service," free of other facts,
wouldn't lead anyone into answering "No," however little the
lawyer knew about the rules of ethics.

So our simple question, without more, wouldn't make a very
good MPRE question. But let's spice it up a bit. Suppose the
lawyer *tells* the client that she's not competent to handle the
matter, but the client insists that she handle it anyway. Say in
addition that the client is the lawyer's biggest client, and that
the client says he'll withdraw all his work if the lawyer doesn't
accept the matter. Getting more interesting, isn't it? Now suppose that the client signs an affidavit acknowledging that the
lawyer has advised him that she doesn't believe she is skilled
enough to handle the matter competently, and promising that he
will not sue her for malpractice regardless of the outcome of the
case. We've embellished the facts, but the "nub" of the matter
is still the same — the lawyer is incompetent to handle the matter. True, there are seemingly relevant new facts — namely, the
client's insistence on the lawyer's handling the work, his waiver
of the right to competent representation, and his agreement not
to sue. An easy question has been transformed into a more challenging one, just by embellishing the facts.

The way to insulate yourself against the trap that's been set for you by these embellishments is to strip them all away and ask yourself what's really going on. Start with the undisputed fact that, underneath it all, the lawyer will provide incompetent service. Then work your way up from there to see if any of the additional facts — here, those additional facts are client consent and waiver — change the nature of that core issue. The answer is "No." A lawyer who provides incompetent service cannot take comfort in client consent. The requirement of competent representation is unqualified and inflexible.

If you maintain your focus in this way, you will make it extremely difficult for the Bar Examiners to confuse you by layering on facts that don't really change the underlying issue.

3. Reading the "Call" of the Question

The "call" of the question contains the instructions that you are expected to follow in choosing among the answers. The call flows logically from the facts, but it can take many forms. It can be very general — for instance, it can ask simply if the attorney's conduct was proper, improper, or subject to discipline — or it can be specific, inquiring into a particular aspect of the attorney's conduct. A specific call is far more common than a general call.

a. "General" call

When a general call is used, the prevailing issue should spring to mind as you read the fact pattern. Here's an example:

Attorney is a member of the bar and a salaried employee of the trust department of Bank. As part of his duties, he prepares a monthly newsletter concerning wills, trusts, estates, and taxes which Bank sends to all of its customers. The newsletter contains a recommendation to the customer to review his or her will in light of the information contained and, if the customer has any questions, to take the will to the bank's trust department where the trust officer will answer any questions without charge. The trust officer is not a lawyer. If the trust officer is unable to answer the customer's questions, the trust officer refers the customer to Attorney.

Is Attorney <u>subject to discipline</u> for the foregoing?

A. Yes, because Attorney is giving legal advice to persons who are not his clients.

B. Yes, because Attorney is aiding Bank in the unauthorized practice of law.

C. No, because no charge is made for Attorney's advice.

D. No, because it is Attorney's duty to carry out Bank's instructions.

As you read this fact pattern, the one fact that should have popped out at you is that Attorney is helping a non-lawyer (Bank) to practice law. The prime issue is the unauthorized practice of law.

If, for whatever reason, you have a problem spotting the issue in a "general call" question, try the following tactic: Rephrase the questions by turning it around. Here, you might ask yourself: "Why *shouldn't* Attorney be subject to discipline on these facts?" Or, "Why *would* he be?"

Take note: If a question asks you whether a particular act is unethical, you can be *pretty* sure that the attorney's done something that fits a particular clause of one of the ethics rules, or one of the exceptions to the rule, or that the conduct itself is unethical — otherwise, the question wouldn't be a very good testing item.

b. "Specific call"

Most MPRE questions call for more specific answers. Example: "Is it proper for Attorney to represent both Catco and Ware in the contempt proceedings?" "Is Attorney subject to discipline if he asserts such a defense?" "Is it proper for Attorney Alpha to supply Judge with the requested list of writings on the subject of custody?" Unlike a general call, the specific call will usually define the issue you're looking for. Let's look at the three questions we've just mentioned and a few more to see how this works.

"Is it proper for Attorney to represent both Catco and Ware in the contempt proceedings?"

The issue here is almost certainly *conflict of interest*, because you're being asked whether it would be proper to represent two people in the same proceeding at the same time.

"Is Attorney subject to discipline if he asserts such a defense?"

Here, the issue probably relates to frivolous claims or to fraud. The Rules specify that an attorney shall not knowingly make a false statement of material fact or law to a tribunal. Model Rule 3.3. They also enjoin a lawyer not to bring or defend a proceeding unless there is a basis for doing so that is not frivolous. Model Rule 3.1.

> "Is it proper for Attorney Alpha to supply Judge with the requested list of writings on the subject of custody?"

The issue here is obviously *ex parte* contact with judges.

> "Is it proper for Attorney Alpha to grant the extension of time without consulting Client?"

The issue is undoubtedly the relative control of the attorney and the client over the process of decisionmaking during the representation or trial. The issue is given away by the words *"without consulting Client."*

If you found this exercise difficult, it's probably because you aren't — not yet, anyway — sufficiently familiar with the Model Rules. Once you've learned them and how they relate to MPRE fact patterns, it will be easier for you to find the issues raised by the Bar Examiners, especially when the call of the question is specific.

c. Spotting the issue when it's not obvious from the fact pattern

In either general or specific call questions, if you can't find the issue in the facts, study the answer options. They will usually give the issue away. Obviously, the right answer will suggest the issue, but at least one or two of the other answers may suggest it, as well. That's because the examiners go to great lengths to craft some of the wrong answers as distractors. These also point to or suggest the main issue, but they manage to elude it, however narrowly. Here's an example:

> Plaintiff and Defendant are next-door neighbors and bitter personal enemies. Plaintiff is suing Defendant over an alleged trespass. Each party believes, in good faith, in the correctness of his position. Plaintiff is represented by Attorney Alpha, and Defendant is represented by Attorney Beta. After Plaintiff had retained Alpha, he told Alpha "I do not want you to grant any delays or courtesies to Defendant or his lawyer. I want you to insist on every technicality."

Alpha has served Beta with a demand to answer written interrogatories. Beta, because of the illness of his secretary, has asked Alpha for a five-day extension of time within which to answer them.

Is Alpha <u>subject to discipline</u> if she grants Beta's request for a five-day extension?

A. Yes, because Alpha is acting contrary to her client's instructions.

B. Yes, unless Alpha first informs Plaintiff of the request and obtains Plaintiff's consent to grant it.

C. No, unless granting the extension would prejudice Plaintiff's rights.

D. No, because Beta was not at fault in causing the delay.

Look carefully at the language in the various answer options here: "granting the extension;" "... Plaintiff's consent;" "... client's instructions." All of them suggest that this is an inquiry into the relative decision-making roles of the lawyer and the client. The best response is C. Why? Because it recognizes that the underlying reason for assigning different levels of control over decisionmaking to the lawyer and the client *is to avoid prejudice to the client's basic rights.* At the same time, it recognizes that lawyers may take such action as is impliedly authorized to carry out representation and that clients normally defer to the special knowledge and skill of their lawyer regarding technical and tactical issues during litigation. Model Rule 1.2, Comments [1] and [2]. The other options are skillful distractors. Answer A suggests that a lawyer always has to get his client's consent on issues of litigation tactics. That is not the case. Answer B is wrong for the same reason as A. Answer D is easy to eliminate. The issue is whether a delay would prejudice Plaintiff's rights, regardless of what caused the delay. Whether Beta was at fault in causing the delay is immaterial to Alpha's decision to grant the request for an extension.

4. Reading the Answers and Choosing the Best Response

As with any standardized test, the best — and sometimes the only — way to arrive at the best response is to eliminate all the options that are *definitely wrong*.

This means that the most important skill you can apply to the MPRE is the ability to perceive when an answer is definitely wrong. There are several ways to hone this skill:

- Learn the general principles for determining when an answer is wrong;

- Review the substantive rules that are most likely to trip you up;

- Learn the traps the Bar Examiners expect you to fall into; and

- Learn how to handle *modifiers.*

We'll teach you all four of these skills in the next few pages. But one point you simply can't ignore is this — the most important element in your success is early and constant review of the Rules themselves. Unlike the LSAT and most other standardized exams, the MPRE is not a test of general intelligence or knowledge. It's based on your intimate knowledge of a specific set of rules which, stripped to their bare bones, cover less than 100 pages of text. That is, it's designed to test your knowledge of a limited subject, and you can't expect to pass it without having at least a reasonable familiarity with the Model Rules and the CJC.

The advice we're going to give you on the next few pages assumes that you've already done your substantive review. (If you haven't done it yet, you'll have to take our word for it when we tell you what the rules are, how they relate to the facts, and how they control your answers.)

Our instructions will do two things for you. First, they'll ensure that you aren't tripped up by the MPRE's format, and that you'll always get the right answer if you know the rule. Also, we'll help you find your way to the right answer when you're not really sure what that answer ought to be. The bottom line is, if you are reasonably familiar with the ethics rules and you apply the principles in this chapter, *the* MPRE *cannot beat you!*

a. General principles of elimination

We've just stated that the most important skill you can take to the MPRE is the ability to identify when an answer is clearly wrong. What makes this more difficult than you may think is the extraordinary skill applied by the examiners in creating the wrong answers. Perhaps you've heard it said that you can tell the quality of a James Bond movie by watching the bad guy — the better the villain, the better the movie. Well, on standardized exams, the better the wrong answers, the more difficult the exam. The MPRE is difficult exactly because the Bar Examiners are exceptionally successful in masking the wrong answers to make them seem right. In this section, we'll show you how to "unmask" the wrong answers and make them easier to spot. Once you know how to eliminate the wrong answers with skill and confidence, you'll be able to pick out the *right* answer every time. Here, then, are the rules you need to know.

(1) If you know the right answer for sure, ignore these instructions.

If there is no question in your mind that one answer is correct, choose it and move on. If you've studied the substance of the Rules and read and practiced with this book, you should find the right answer on a first or second reading. If you do spot the right answer right away, mark your answer sheet and go on to the next question.

(2) Eliminate any answers you know are wrong, and then concentrate on the remaining answer choices.

In many cases you will immediately recognize that at least one and perhaps two of the answer choices are wrong. If you can spot three, great — you're left with the one option that has to be right. Don't bother to look a second time at answer options that are clearly wrong; cross them off in your test booklet if necessary to take your mind off them, and concentrate on the other possibilities.

(3) Remember that many of the answers will seem to draw on the same issue.

This rule isn't set in stone, but the nature of the exam makes it likely that several answers will focus on the same issue. Remember, what makes a standardized test difficult is the seeming resemblance between the *wrong* answers and the *right* one. This leads to one simple rule: *in general*, if there is a single answer option that seems very different from the other options, it's probably not the best answer.

(4) Analyze the ways in which a particular answer can be wrong.

There are several clues to concluding that an answer is wrong. An answer is wrong if:

(a) It misapplies a rule of ethics to the facts. This is far and away the most common type of distractor; we discuss this in detail under "Traps Set by the Bar Examiners."

(b) It misstates the ethics rules. This is also relatively common.

(c) It misstates or deliberately confuses the facts. An answer of this kind is so clearly wrong that it fools only the least prepared applicants; for this reason, it's not used very often.

b. A few general rules to remember

Here are a few general rules you should keep in mind. They will save you a lot of time in choosing the right answer.

(1) Don't be confused by a question which suggests that the lawyer's conduct, though questionable, has not prejudiced the client.

This is a very common MPRE trap—the facts describe conduct by a lawyer that is wrong, but then tell us that the misconduct has not affected the client adversely. When this happens in an MPRE fact pattern, you can bet your bottom dollar that at least one of the distractors will suggest that the lawyer's conduct was proper because his client wasn't "prejudiced," or "adversely affected," or the like. For this reason, it's important to keep the following basic rule in mind—even if things work out all right for the client, the lawyer may still be subject to discipline for violating the rules in the first place. To avoid picking the wrong answer in this kind of question, you need to know the Model Rules in all their subtleties. (Note: *To recover in a malpractice case, the client has to show not only that the lawyer's conduct was negligent or improper, but that the conduct was the direct cause of the client's loss or injury.*)

Let's look at an example. Say a lawyer allows a paralegal in his office to conduct a deposition or perform some other act that constitutes the practice of law. The lawyer will be subject to discipline for assisting a person who is not a member of the bar in the unauthorized practice of law (Model Rule 5.5(a)) *even if* that person renders competent service. Let's try another one. Suppose a lawyer neglects the client's work over an extended period; he may be subject to discipline *even if* he finally manages to file the client's claim before the Statute of Limitations runs out. (He may have neglected to pursue an earlier opportunity to settle the matter, for example.)

See what I mean? This kind of behavior is analogous to a crime such as burglary: once a person's broken into a dwelling at night with the intent to commit a felony, it doesn't matter what he does after that — he can change his mind and exit without touching anything — he's still guilty of burglary. It's the same with some lawyer infractions. Once a lawyer has engaged in unethical conduct, it doesn't really matter what the consequence of that conduct is to the client; the lawyer has violated the ethics rules and he's subject to discipline.

(2) When it comes to fees, less is better

Occasionally the MPRE will ask about the propriety of a fee that is in dispute. Remember that the Model Rules specify that a lawyer's fee shall be reasonable (Model Rule 1.5(a)); it's a safe bet, therefore, that less will be perceived as more reasonable than more. Thus, when a question asks what part of a fee a lawyer may properly keep, you're generally safe if you opt for the choice that best protects the client's interests in the money under dispute. Here's an example:

Deft retained Attorney to appeal Deft's criminal conviction and to seek bail pending appeal. The agreed fee for the appearance on the bail hearing was $50 per hour. Attorney received $800 from Deft, of which $300 was a deposit to secure Attorney's fee and $500 was for bail costs in the event that bail was obtained. Attorney maintained two office bank accounts: a "Fee Account," in which all fees were deposited and from which all office expenses were paid, and a "Client Fund Account." Attorney deposited the $800 in the "Client Fund Account" and expended six hours of time on the bail hearing. The effort to obtain bail was unsuccessful. Dissatisfied, Deft immediately demanded return of the $800.

It is now <u>proper</u> for Attorney to:

A. transfer the $800 to the "Fee Account."

B. transfer $300 to the "Fee Account" and leave $500 in the "Client Fund Account" until Attorney's fee for the final appeal is determined.

C. transfer $300 to the "Fee Account" and send Deft a $500 check on the "Client Fund Account."

D. send Deft a $500 check and leave $300 in the "Client Fund Account" until the matter is resolved with Deft.

With no other thought in mind than the general rule that "less for the lawyer, more for the client" is better than the alternative, you can see that the best response would have to be D, because it's the one in which Attorney gets to keep less than he does in any other response.

(3) If a rule forbids communication between two persons, it doesn't matter who initiates the communication.

The Model Rules contain many provisions that forbid communication between a lawyer and someone else. Examples: A lawyer shall not communicate with a person he knows to be represented by another attorney without that attorney's consent (Model Rule 4.2); a lawyer shall not communicate *ex parte* with a judge, juror, or prospective juror (Model Rule 3.5); a lawyer shall not contact or solicit professional employment either in-person or by live telephone from any person who is not a family member or former client (Model Rule 7.3).

The rule to remember is that when communication by a lawyer is banned, it's banned in almost every instance regardless of who contacts whom first. (Except, of course, that the lawyer may discuss a matter with a prospective client who initiates the contact.) Thus, for instance, if a juror tries to strike up a conversation with one of the lawyers in a case, the lawyer has to terminate the conversation immediately. It's quite common on the MPRE for a distractor to suggest that a communication is proper because someone other than the lawyer in the fact pattern initiated the contact. Don't be fooled by this device!

(4) An attorney may not engage in conduct that would cause a judge to violate the Code of Judicial Conduct.

Sometimes an MPRE fact pattern will point to a judge who has violated the Code of Judicial Conduct with the help of a lawyer. A common example concerns a judge who contacts a lawyer because she happens to be an expert on a particular issue in a litigation, instead of relying solely on the briefs submitted by counsel.

While there's nothing in the Model Rules that discourages a lawyer from advising a judge on the law, the CJC itself requires that a judge refrain from relying on the advice unless the judge first tells the lawyers in the case the name of the expert consulted and the substance of her advice, and gives the lawyers a chance to respond. CJC Canon 3(7)(b). Remember, therefore, that it's not enough to know the Model Rules. When a judge is involved, you have to include the CJC in your analysis of a lawyer's conduct. Under Model Rule 8.4(f), a lawyer can't knowingly aid a judge in violating the law *or the CJC*. Thus, if a judge's conduct violates the CJC and a lawyer has helped the judge in that conduct, the lawyer has violated the ethics rules.

(5) A client's insistence on a course of conduct doesn't relieve the lawyer of the responsibility to observe the Rules.

Sometimes an MPRE fact pattern will feature an attorney who has violated the Rules at the insistence of the client — e.g., asserting an unmeritorious or baseless claim for the sake of harassing the adversary, or taking on work when the lawyer isn't competent to handle it. Rule to remember: the client's insistence on improper conduct by the lawyer doesn't relieve the lawyer of the obligation not to engage in the conduct.

c. Traps set by the Bar Examiners

Knowing the tricks the Bar Examiners use to lure you into choosing the wrong answer can save you from the temptation to pick them instead of the right answer. When the Bar Examiners create an MPRE, their central concern is to preserve the integrity of the exam. They want people who know the Rules to pass the exam, and people who don't know the Rules, to fail.

(In fact, this is the only way they can convince the states to include the exam as part of their licensing requirements.) So what they do is to set "traps" for the unwary.

It's almost as though they deliberately calculate and anticipate the mistakes students are likely to make and build around them. They design and construct "distractors" — wrong answers — precisely to lure everyone into making these very mistakes.

(1) The "Hmmm, that sounds familiar" trap

This is the most common — and most insidious — trap on the MPRE. Many law students have a tendency to review for exams only until they can respond by rote. They don't bother to analyze the material to the point of real understanding, and they especially don't bother to apply the material to real facts. The MPRE examiners know this about law students, so they construct answers that seem right because they correctly state a rule or a part of a rule — EXCEPT THAT the rule they state is not the rule that applies to the facts. Here's an example:

> Attorney represented Landlord in a variety of matters over several years. Plaint, an elderly widow living on public assistance, filed suit against Landlord alleging that Landlord withheld without justification the security deposit on a rental unit that Plaint vacated three years ago. She brought the action for herself, without counsel, in small claims court. Attorney investigated the claim and learned that it was legally barred by the applicable statute of limitations, although Plaint's underlying claim was meritorious. Attorney told Landlord of the legal defense, but emphasized that Plaint's claim was just and that, in all fairness, the security deposit should be returned to Plaint. Attorney told Landlord:
>
>> "I strongly recommend that you pay Plaint the full amount with interest. It is against your long-term business interests to be known in the community as a landlord who routinely withholds security deposits even though the tenant leaves the apartment in good condition. Paying the claim now will prevent future headaches for you."

Was Attorney's conduct <u>proper</u>?

A. Yes, if Landlord did not object to Attorney's advice and paid Plaint's claim.

B. Yes, because Attorney may refer to both legal and nonlegal considerations in advising a client.

C. No, unless Attorney's engagement letter informed Landlord that Attorney's advice on the matter would include both legal and nonlegal considerations.

D. No, because in advising Landlord to pay the full claim, Attorney failed to represent zealously Landlord's legal interests.

Look at option D. This is a tempting choice because it sounds familiar; you may even say to yourself, "I've seen something like this in one of the Rules, so it must be right." The problem is, the language used — the responsibility of a lawyer to act with zeal — is not what the facts are getting at.

Choice D is wrong because it's not directed at whether Attorney's advice, which went beyond purely technical legal advice, was proper, and that's the issue here.

Option C does the same thing, but this time it suggests a different but equally inapplicable Rule. The idea of an engagement letter will ring a bell, but such letter to the client is concerned with fees. Its purpose is to make clear what services the lawyer will provide and what she will charge for them, not in what form she will render advice. Model Rule 1.5.

See how tempting it is to choose one of these answers? They reference the Rules in a way that is familiar, and unless you realize that the pivotal issue here concerns the appropriate scope of a lawyer's advice to a client, you might choose C or D. Don't think Bar Examiners don't realize this when they create answer options like this! (Incidentally, the best response is B. A lawyer should exercise professional judgment and give candid advice, which may rely on considerations other than purely technical legal advice.)

The only way to insulate yourself against this kind of trap is to study and know the Rules. If you are sufficiently familiar with the Rules, you'll be able to distinguish one Rule from another.

(2) Stating part of a rule, and omitting a part that would change the result

A frequent trick in distractors is the partial statement of a rule, or the statement of a rule without including a relevant or controlling exception. Let's look at an example.

> Attorney filed an action on behalf of Client for breach of contract. In fact, Client had no legal basis for the suit, but wanted to harass Defendant. In order, to induce Attorney to file the action. Client made certain false statements of material fact to Attorney, which Attorney included in the complaint filed against Defendant.
>
> At the trial of the case, Client took the stand and testified as set forth in the complaint. The trial court ordered judgment for Client. After entry of judgment, Client wrote Attorney a letter marked "Confidential," in which Client admitted that she had lied to Attorney and had testified falsely in the case.
>
> Upon complaint of Defendant, who claimed Attorney had knowingly used false testimony in the case of Client v. Defendant, disciplinary proceedings were instituted against Attorney.
>
> Is it <u>proper</u> for Attorney to use Client's letter to Attorney in Attorney's defense in the disciplinary proceedings?
>
> **A.** Yes, if it is necessary to do so in order to protect Attorney's rights.
>
> **B.** Yes, because Client had committed a fraud on the court in which the case was tried.
>
> **C.** No, because Attorney learned the facts from Client in confidence.
>
> **D.** No, if disclosure by Attorney could result in Client's prosecution for perjury.

Look at option C. It suggests the *general* rule prohibiting a lawyer from revealing any information relating to the representation of a client without the client's consent, but it ignores the *exception* to this rule, which is core to these facts. The exception is that a lawyer *may reveal* a client confidence in order to defend himself in a controversy with the client, to defend himself against a criminal charge or civil claim for conduct involving the client, or to respond to allegations in any proceeding concerning the representation. Model Rule 1.6a. Thus, *whenever* an answer option seems to state a prevailing rule, be on your guard — don't accept the statement at face value — scan your memory to verify that the rule has been stated either completely or in *pertinent* part, and pay special attention to all the exceptions you know.

(3) Focusing on an issue that wasn't addressed in the "call" of the question

Sometimes when you read a fact pattern on the MPRE, an issue you've learned well will jump off the page at you. You'll immediately assume that's the issue the question is focusing on. But don't let yourself be distracted. Focus *only* on what's asked in the *call* of the question. If it's a specific call, and it doesn't elicit the issue that first jumped out at you, you can be sure that one of the distractors will rely on that very issue — and, of course, it's one of the three wrong answers. (Remember, this rule applies only to questions following a *specific* call. If the call of the question is general — e.g., "Is Attorney subject to discipline for his conduct?" — then the issue you first spotted may well be the basis for the correct answer.)

d. Modifiers can lead you to the best response

Remember that the basic format for MPRE answer options looks like this: "*No, if* Psy is not compensated in any way for referring cases to Attorney." The first word, "Yes" or "No," states the *result*. The word immediately after the comma is the *modifier*. And the remainder of the answer is the *reasoning behind the result*. Your instinct will tell you that the reasoning is the most important part of the answer option. But frequently that one-word modifier — the "if," "unless," or "because" immediately after the comma — is as important as the reasoning itself! Learning how to analyze answers based on their modifiers will dramatically improve your chances of answering any MPRE question correctly. And that's what we'll explain to you here.

The examiners use three kinds of modifiers on the MPRE — "because," "if," and "unless." Let's look at how each one affects the meaning of the answer.

(1) The definite modifier — "because"

"Because" is a *definite*, as opposed to a *conditional*, modifier. Simply put, when "because" is the modifier, it must *necessarily* be true that the reasoning leads to the result. In order for an answer beginning with "because" to be correct, the following three elements must exist.

(a) Resolve central issue

The reasoning must address and resolve an issue central to the call of the question — or, at least, an issue more central than any other response.

(b) Unequivocally reflect facts

The facts in the reasoning must *completely* and *unequivocally* confirm the facts in the basic fact pattern. For instance, if an option states, "because there was a conflict between two of his clients, Alpha and Beta," the facts must *clearly* show a conflict between Alpha and Beta.

(c) Agreement between result and reasoning

The result must be consistent with the reasoning. For instance, if the reasoning tells you, "because the representation was competent," the result must be that the representation is proper. Although keep in mind that if the lawyer's competence isn't the central issue, this element *alone* will not necessarily make the option the best response.

This is pretty technical stuff. Let's look at an example to illustrate what we're talking about.

> Four years ago, Alpha was a judge in a state court of general jurisdiction and heard the civil case of Plaintiff against Defendant. Plaintiff prevailed and secured a judgment for $50,000 which was sustained on appeal. Since then Alpha has resigned from the bench and returned to private practice. Defendant has filed suit to enjoin enforcement of the judgment on the grounds of extrinsic fraud in its procurement. Plaintiff has now asked Alpha to represent Plaintiff in defending the suit to enjoin enforcement.
>
> Is it proper for Alpha to accept the representation of Plaintiff in this matter?

A. Yes, because Alpha would be upholding the decision of the court.

B. Yes, if Alpha's conduct of the first trial will not be in issue.

C. No, unless Alpha believes the present suit is brought in bad faith.

D. No, because Alpha had acted in a judicial capacity on the merits of the original case.

Let's look at option D, a "because" answer option. By the time you read option D, you should have determined that the *problem* here is the conflict of interest that can arise when a lawyer moves from the judiciary to private practice. The rule is that a lawyer can't represent anyone in connection with a matter in which the lawyer participated personally and substantially as a judge, unless all parties to the proceeding give informed, written consent. Model Rule 1.12(a).

Now, let's go through the three elements for the "because" modifier to see if D is correct. Remember, our shorthand for those three elements is: (1) resolves a central issue; (2) unequivocally reflects the facts; and (3) shows agreement between result and reasoning.

First, does option D address and resolve a central issue? Yes, it does; the issue is whether Alpha can properly represent Plaintiff, and this turns on whether his conflict of interest prevents him from doing so. D cites the rule on conflicts of interest for former judges, the central issue, so D passes the first hurdle.

The second hurdle is determining whether the reasoning unequivocally reflects the facts. It does. You're told that Alpha was the judge in Plaintiff v. Defendant, and the new suit deals with the enforceability of that judgment. Thus, as option D indicates, Alpha did in fact participate "personally and substantially" as judge in the original case.

Finally, the result and the reasoning must agree. Because the reasoning in D is true, then a conflict of interest must exist that would prevent Alpha from representing

Plaintiff. Option D tells you that it would not be proper for Alpha to represent Plaintiff under these facts. Thus, the result and the reasoning agree. (Note, incidentally, that representing Plaintiff would not only be improper — it would subject Alpha to discipline; but, then, every disciplinable act or omission is necessarily improper.)

Now that you've seen how you can determine if a "because" option is correct, let's see how you can conclude that some "because" answers are *incorrect*. Look at option A, which also begins with the modifier "because." Let's look directly at the three "hurdles," the first one first. Does the reasoning of the option address and resolve a central issue? *No*. The central issue is conflict, so it doesn't matter whether Alpha is upholding his decision or not; what matters is that he was acting as judge in the first trial and that this creates an irreconcilable conflict in the second trial. Because option A fails to clear the first hurdle, you can move on to the next option; you've eliminated A as an acceptable response.

If you have difficulty determining whether a "because" option is correct, there is a way that may help you. Combine the reasoning of the answer with the call of the question to create an "if-then" statement. If the "if-then" statement is true, the answer is correct. If we do this with answer A, we wind up with the following statement: "If Alpha is upholding the decision of the court, then it would be proper for Alpha to represent Plaintiff." As you can see, the "if" clause is the reasoning in the original answer, and the "then" statement restates the call of the question. In order for the statement to be true, the "if" clause must provide a valid reason for the resulting "then" element. In answer A, it doesn't — the fact that Alpha isn't challenging the judgment doesn't resolve the conflict of interest in favor of his representing Plaintiff. If you're stuck on a "because" option, try rewording it in this way to help clarify whether or not it's correct.

Incidentally, did you notice what kind of a "distractor" option A is? It's one in which the reasoning evokes a rule that seems correct but *doesn't apply* to the facts. Option A evokes the lawyer's duty of loyalty to former clients — i.e., the Rule that states a lawyer can't represent a new client with interests adverse to a former client in a substantially related matter. Model Rule 1.9(a). (For instance, a lawyer can't seek to rescind on behalf of a new client a contract he drafted for an old client, or challenge the validity of a will for a descendant that he prepared and witnessed for the decedent.) Option A suggests that because Alpha isn't challenging his own judgment, his representation of Plaintiff is proper. Of course, this is wrong, because the conflict exists *independently* of whether Alpha is challenging his own decision. Nonetheless, you can see why the evocation of another rule makes A a good distractor.

(2) The conditional modifiers: — "if" and "unless"

"If" and "unless" are called conditional responses, because the result is conditional on the reasoning. Unlike the Multistate Bar Exam (MBE) — where "if" and "unless" responses are rare — these are very common on the MPRE. This is because the rules governing ethics and professionalism are more fact-dependent than are the more substantive rules tested on the MBE.

When you see "if" or "unless" as a modifier in an answer option, the reasoning will do one of two things:

— It will clarify ambiguous facts in the fact pattern; or

— It will add facts which resolve a central issue.

Let's look at each modifier separately to see how you should analyze questions that use them.

(a) When "if" is the modifier

In order for an "if" option to be the best response, it must overcome these three hurdles:

(1) Plausibility

The reasoning must be *plausible* on the facts — that is, there can't be anything in the facts to suggest the statement *cannot* be true. (Of course, this also means that the reasoning can't be *unequivocally* established by the facts, either.) Let's say the issue in an MPRE question is incompetence, and you're told that

Attorney went on a three-month drunken binge and neglected to file his client's complaint before the Statute of Limitations ran out. If the call of the question asked you whether Attorney was subject to discipline, the response would not be correct if it said, "Yes, *if* he rendered incompetent representation," because the facts show that Attorney's conduct was *unquestionably* incompetent; there's no realistic way to deem Attorney's service competent, so the statement can't be considered plausible.

(2) Central issue

The reasoning must address a *central issue*. In order for an "if" option to be correct, it must either add essential facts or clarify existing facts in such a way as to resolve a central issue. The easiest way to show what this means is with an example.

The law firm of Alpha and Beta has a radio commercial which states:

"Do you have a legal problem? Are you being sued? Consult Alpha and Beta, licensed attorneys at law. Initial conference charge is $25 for one hour. Act now and protect your interests. Call at 1234 Main Street; telephone area code (101) 123-4567."

Are Alpha and Beta *subject to discipline* for the commercial?

A. Yes, because the qualifications of the lawyers are not stated.

B. Yes, because the radio broadcast may encourage litigation.

C. No, if all the statements in the radio broadcast are true.

D. No, unless the radio broadcast is heard outside the state in which they are licensed.

Is Attorney *subject to discipline* in State First?

Let's look at option C. Remember our first two hurdles — plausibility and central issue. The first hurdle option C must clear in order to be the best response is to be *plausible* under the facts.The facts tell you that Alpha and Beta have a radio commercial and give you the content of the commercial. Thus, it's plausible — neither definite nor impossible — that the statements in the commercial are true, so option C clears the first hurdle.

Now we have to see if it clears the second hurdle — namely, does option C address a *central issue* raised by the facts? To do that, we have to step back a minute and call up the rule that is evoked by these facts. The issue is whether the advertisement is acceptable under Model Rule 7.2, which allows a lawyer to advertise by any public medium or through written or recorded media. Rule 7.2 is subject to Model Rule 7.1, however, which requires that the advertisement not be false or misleading.

The facts do not tell you whether the statements in the advertisement are false or misleading, but option C supplies that essential fact. In doing do, it resolves the central issue.

(3) Agreement between result and reasoning

The result and the reasoning must agree. If we conclude that an "if" option is plausible under the facts and that it resolves a central issue in the facts, it still has one last hurdle to clear: the result — before the comma introducing "if" — and the reasoning — after the comma following "if" — must agree. In our sample problem, if the statements are true Alpha and Beta will not be subject to discipline. Because the call of the question asks you if they'll be subject to discipline, the result would have to be "no." Since it is, option C must be the best response — and it is.

Note that if the reasoning stated the opposite fact, the result would also have to state the opposite in order for option C to be correct. That is, if the reasoning were "The statements weren't true," then the result would have to be "yes" in order for the option to be correct. So if you reversed both the result and the reasoning in option C, it would say, "yes, if the statements were false." Incidentally, note that in this reverse form option C *still* would also be correct because: it would be plausible under the facts, it would resolve a central issue, and its result and reasoning would agree.

(b) When "unless" is the modifier

Like "if," "unless" is a conditional modifier. In fact, "if" and "unless" are *almost* mirror images of each other. (But note one difference between them — a correct "if" response provides circumstances under which the result might occur; when "unless" is the modifier, the *reasoning must provide the only circumstance under which the result would not occur* before the option can be the best response.) For instance, if the call of the question asks you whether an attorney's conduct is proper, and an answer option begins "No, unless," the reasoning must provide the only way that would make the attorney's conduct proper. If instead, the call of the question asks you whether an attorney is subject to discipline, and an answer option begins, "Yes, unless," the reasoning of that option must supply the only way that enables an attorney to *avoid* discipline. If you can think of even *one other way* in which the same result could occur, an option containing "unless" *cannot* be the best response.

As with "if" answers, the reasoning in a correct "unless" response will either clarify the facts in the fact pattern, or provide an additional fact that resolves a central issue. Let's look at an example:

Attorney Alpha was retained by Client to incorporate Client's business, which previously had been operated as a sole proprietorship. Alpha noticed in Client's file copies of some correspondence from Client to Attorney Beta concerning the possibility of Beta's incorporating Client's business. Alpha questioned Client to make certain that any attorney-client relationship between Beta and Client had been terminated. Client told Alpha,

"It certainly has been terminated. When I discussed the matter with Beta six months ago, he asked for a retainer of $1,000, which I paid him. He did absolutely nothing after he got the money, even though I called him weekly, and finally, last week when I again complained, he returned the retainer. But don't say anything about it because Beta is an old friend of my family."

Is Alpha subject to discipline if she does not report her knowledge of Beta's conduct to the appropriate authority?

A. Yes, if Alpha believes Beta clearly was guilty of professional misconduct.

B. Yes, unless Alpha believes Beta does not usually neglect matters entrusted to him.

C. No, if Client was satisfied by Beta's return of the retainer.

D. No, unless Client agrees that Alpha may report the information.

Look at option D. When you read the call of this question, you should have recognized that the issue was whether or not Alpha was required to report Beta's misconduct. You should also have summoned to mind the rule on a lawyer's duty to report another lawyer's violation of the Model Rules of Professional Conduct if the violation raises a substantial question as to that lawyer's honesty, trustworthiness, or fitness as a lawyer. When information about the violation is protected under the confidentiality rules of Model Rule 1.6, however, the duty becomes discretionary rather than absolute. If the client whose confidentiality would be breached does not give consent to the disclosure, a lawyer need not report the violation.

Option D provides the only situation in which Alpha would not be subject to discipline if she does not report Beta's conduct to the appropriate authority.

Remember how a couple of paragraphs back, we said, that "unless" and "if" were *almost* mirror images? Let's change option D a little bit to see how this works. Say option D, instead of "No, unless..." said "Yes, if Client, has agreed that Alpha may report the information." Note that the reasoning is plausible, it addresses and resolves a central issue, and the reasoning and the result agree. Thus, "if" makes option D correct in the same way as "unless."

Keep in mind, however, that "if" and "unless" aren't perfect mirror images, because "unless" requires exclusivity, and "if" doesn't. Looking at our option D with "if" as the modifier, you can see that it's offering one way in which Attorney's conduct would be made proper — getting the client's consent — but it doesn't exclude other ways. On the other hand, when "No, unless..." begins the option, the reasoning that follows states the only way in which the result could occur; in other words, it states the only way for Attorney to avoid discipline on these facts. A perfect mirror image of "unless," then, would not be "if" alone, but "if and only if."

This whole discourse on modifiers, and exactly what they mean, may strike you as overly technical when applied to such simple words as "if" and "unless." Be assured, however, if you're thoroughly familiar with our method for analyzing modifiers, you'll be well on your way to avoiding the wrong answers.

E. The EZ-Pass to the Right Answer

Learning how to analyze answers correctly can do more for you than simply help you avoid pitfalls. If you put to work all of the principles we've discussed here, you'll frequently be able to pick the right answer to an MPRE question on first reading! Of course, you shouldn't rush to judgment, because the MPRE is an important exam, but the point is that you can learn to increase your confidence and trust your instincts. Your ability to do this is built on something we mentioned earlier — namely, the tension between the flexibility inherent in the ethics rules and the need for concrete answers to standardized multi-choice questions. As a result of this tension, the answer options often contain so many qualifying facts that they lead you inexorably to the one best choice. Let's look at a few examples of how this works. Here are the four answer options to a past MPRE question:

A. Yes, unless Alpha's time was completely occupied with work for other clients.

B. Yes, because Alpha neglected the representation of Passenger.

C. No, because Passenger's suit was filed before the statute of limitations ran.

D. No, because Alpha returned the $1,000 retainer to Passenger.

Without first having read the corresponding fact pattern, you should be able to guess the best response. A quick glance at each of the options should tell you that the facts probably revolve around a lawyer who didn't act promptly enough in representing her client. Remember, good distractors often focus on the same issue as the best response does. This should suggest to you that the issue raised by the fact pattern requires an analysis of the standard set by Mode Rule 1.3 to determine whether a lawyer has acted diligently and promptly in representing the client. You know that the rule requires a lawyer to act with "reasonable diligence and promptness." You also know that a lawyer should control her workload to avoid neglecting one client in favor of others and that unreasonable delay is unacceptable even if the client's interests are not affected in substance. That makes it easy to eliminate options A and C. Option D cannot be the right answer because the issue is neglect of Passenger's interests not the retainer. With all of that in mind, the best answer is almost certainly option B.

To prove the validity of our approach here are the facts to this same question:

Attorney Alpha was retained by Passenger, a passenger on a bus, who had been injured in a collision between the bus and a truck. Passenger paid Alpha a retainer of $1,000 and agreed further that Alpha should have a fee of 25% of any recovery before filing suit, 30% of any recovery after suit was filed but before judgment, and 35% of any recovery after trial and judgment. Alpha promptly called the lawyer for the bus company and told him she was representing Passenger and would like to talk about a settlement. Alpha made an appointment to talk to the lawyer for the bus company but did not keep the appointment. Alpha continued to put off talking to the lawyer for the bus company. Meanwhile, Passenger became concerned because she had heard nothing from Alpha. Passenger called Alpha's office but was told Alpha was not in and would not call back. Passenger was told not to worry because Alpha would look after her interests. After ten months had passed, Passenger went to Attorney Beta for advice. Beta advised Passenger that the statute of limitations would run in one week and, with Passenger's consent, immediately filed suit for Passenger. Alpha, upon Passenger's demand, refunded the $1,000 Passenger had paid.

Is Alpha <u>subject to discipline</u>?

As you can see, the facts confirm that B is the best response. This should give you the confidence to trust your instincts as you measure the answer options under facts such as these. Let's try another one. Here are the four answer options.

A. Yes, because Attorney has no interest in the case.

B. Yes, if Judge believes that Attorney's advice is needed to serve the interests of justice.

C. No, unless all parties in the case first give their written consent to Judge's consultation with Attorney.

D. No, unless Judge informs the parties of Attorney's identity and the substance of Attorney's advice, and asks for their responses.

Let's try to deduce what facts lie behind these options. We can logically assume that Judge has consulted Attorney (who is probably not an attorney for one of the parties — option A tells us that he has no interest in the case. That's implied by all of the answer options, and, as you know by now, distractors are only effective if they contain elements common to the correct answer. Judicial Canon 3(B)(7)(b) is at issue here. It permits a judge to consult a disinterested party on applicable law providing she follows certain guidelines. The answer options should tell you that the fact pattern probably concerns a judge who asked an uninterested party for advice concerning a proceeding before her and that option D is probably the best answer.

> Judge is presiding in a case that has, as its main issue, a complicated point of commercial law. The lawyers have not presented the case to Judge's satisfaction, and Judge believes she needs additional legal advice. Judge's former partner in law practice, Attorney, is an expert in the field of law that is at issue. Attorney has no interest in the case.
>
> Is it <u>proper</u> for Judge to consult Attorney?

As you can see, reading the facts, as in our last example, only reinforces your judgment that the best answer is option D. Let's try one more set of options.

A. Yes, because Client instructed Attorney not to tell anyone about the jewelry box.

B. Yes, if the disclosure would be detrimental to Client's interests.

C. No, because the jewelry box was not involved in the dispute between Client and Partner.

D. No, if the disclosure is necessary to enable Attorney to defend against a criminal charge.

Looking at these options, you can reasonably assume that the facts revolve around confidentiality. A lawyer has a duty not to reveal information relating to the representation of a client without the client's consent. Model Rule 1.6(a). An exception to the rule, however, is the lawyer's right to defend herself against a criminal charge based upon conduct in which the client was involved. Model Rule 1.6(b)(5). Because option D clearly outlines this exception to the client-confidentiality rule, it is very likely the best answer.

The facts to this question bear this out:

> Attorney had been representing Client for several months in a matter involving the ownership of some antique jewelry. Client claimed he purchased the jewelry for his wife with his own funds. Partner, Client's business partner, claimed the jewelry was a partnership purchase in which he, Partner, had a one-half interest. While the matter was pending, Client brought a valuable antique jewelry box to Attorney's office and said:
>
>> "Keep this in your vault for me. I bought it before I went into business with Partner. Do not tell him or anyone else about it until my matter with Partner is settled."

Later that same day, a police officer, who was in Attorney's office on another matter, saw the jewelry box when a clerk opened the vault to put in some papers. The police officer recognized it as one that had recently been stolen from a collector. Attorney was arrested and later charged with receiving stolen property.

Is Attorney <u>subject to discipline</u> if Attorney reveals that Client brought the box to her office?

We could go on like this, but you've got the point by now — if you are sufficiently well-versed in analyzing answer options to MPRE questions and relating them to the facts, you'll be so well prepared for the MPRE that you could well pass the exam just by reasoning your way through the options without reading the questions! But don't get the wrong idea. We're emphasizing the skills you will have developed, not the tactics you should use on the exam. We're not recommending that you skip the facts.

On the contrary, we recommend that you read and reread every fact pattern before you consider the options. And then trust the skills and the instinct you've developed by reviewing and understanding the rules, studying this little book and reasoning your way to the right answers.

Good luck.

Part Two

Model Questions and Answers

In Part One, I did all the work. Here in Part Two, we'll share the load. This Part contains 50 questions reproduced verbatim from the booklet, **MPRE Sample Questions VI**, published by the National Conference of Bar Examiners. With these model questions, you should be able to put into practice the plan of attack you learned in Part One. The 50 model questions are followed by my explanation and analysis of the answer options. My answers begin on page 78 and reflect the Model Rules of Professional Conduct (1993 code, as amended through August 2003) and the Code of Judicial Conduct (1990 code, as amended through August 2003.

Your job is to read the question and then pick the right answer. See if you agree both with my answer and my reasoning.

A couple of brief words of advice before you get started. First of all, don't pay attention to timing as you read. On the real MPRE, you'll have about two minutes, on average, for each question. But put that out of your mind for now. When you practice here, it's much more important to pay attention to applying the principles from Part One than to beat the clock. Speed will come naturally as you become more proficient at reading the questions and choosing among the answers.

Also, if you pick the wrong answer option, don't stop after you read the correct response; read why the option you chose is wrong. (It's a good idea to make note of these "near misses" as you answer the questions). Each response is designed to show you not only the correct rule, but, far more importantly, the mistake you made when you chose the wrong response. You may actually learn more from analyzing the wrong answer than from reviewing the right answer!

In terms of breaking up the questions, do whatever makes you feel comfortable. My guess is that you'd be wise to do 10 or so model questions, check your results, and then proceed. Breaking your review down into small chunks like this, and reviewing answers as you go, gives you a chance to identify and correct any flaws you make before they become habits. But if you feel very confident from the start, there's no reason why you can't just do all 50 questions at once, and then review the answers.

With all this in mind — let's get started.

A. Model Questions

Question 1.

State does not require lawyers to participate in continuing legal education courses. Attorneys Alpha, Beta, and Gamma, all lawyers recently admitted to practice, formed a law partnership in State. As they considered what expenses the partnership would pay on behalf of each lawyer, a majority decided that the firm would not pay for continuing legal education courses since they were not required by State. Gamma, who wanted reimbursement for continuing legal education courses, angrily said, "Fine, I won't attend any continuing legal education courses."

Is it proper for Gamma to refuse to attend any continuing legal education courses?

A. Yes, unless the state offers free continuing legal education courses.

B. Yes, if Gamma independently undertakes continuing study and education in the law.

C. No, because Gamma cannot maintain competence without attending continuing legal education courses.

D. No, unless Gamma obtains malpractice insurance.

Question 2.

Client, a new client of Attorney, has asked Attorney to write a letter recommending Client's nephew for admission to the bar. Client has told Attorney that he has no direct contact with the nephew, but that Client's sister (the nephew's mother) has assured Client that the nephew is industrious and honest.

Which of the following would be proper for Attorney?

I.   Write the letter on the basis of Client's assurance.

II. Write the letter on the basis of Client's assurance if Attorney has no unfavorable information about the nephew.

III. Make an independent investigation and write the letter only if Attorney is thereafter satisfied that the nephew is qualified.

A. III only

B. I and II, but not III

C. I and III, but not II

D. I, II, and III

Question 3.

Alpha is a member of the bar in State First and is also licensed as a stockbroker in State Second. In his application for renewal of his stockbroker's license in State Second, Alpha knowingly filed a false financial statement.

Is Alpha subject to discipline in State First for so doing?

A. Yes, because his actions involve dishonesty or misrepresentation.

B. Yes, but only if he is first convicted of a criminal offense in State Second.

C. No, because his action was not in his capacity as an attorney.

D. No, because his action was not in State First.

Question 4.

Attorney is a sole practitioner whose practice is largely in the areas of tax, wills, estates, and trusts. Attorney learned of a new Internal Revenue Service (IRS) regulation that probably affects the trust provisions in a will she prepared for Testatrix two years ago. Attorney has not represented Testatrix since she drew the will.

Is Attorney subject to discipline if she calls to Testatrix and advises her of the new IRS ruling and the need to revise the will?

A. Yes, if Attorney has any reason to believe that Testatrix has another lawyer.

B. Yes, because Attorney would be soliciting legal business from a person who is not a current client.

C. No, provided Attorney does not thereafter prepare a new will for Testatrix.

D. No, because Testatrix is a former client of Attorney.

Question 5.

Deft retained Attorney to appeal Deft's criminal conviction and to seek bail pending appeal. The agreed fee for the appearance on the bail hearing was $50 per hour. Attorney received $800 from Deft of which $300 was a deposit to secure Attorney's fee and $500 was for bail costs in the event that bail was obtained. Attorney maintained two office bank accounts: a "Fee Account," in which all fees were deposited and from which all office expenses were paid, and a "Clients' Fund Account." Attorney deposited the $800 in the "Clients' Fund Account" the week before the bail hearing. Attorney expended six hours of time on the bail hearing. The effort to obtain bail was unsuccessful. Dissatisfied, Deft immediately demanded return of the $800.

It is now <u>proper</u> for Attorney to:

A. transfer the $800 to the "Fee Account."

B. transfer $300 to the "Fee Account" and leave $500 in the "Clients' Fund Account" until Attorney's fee for the final appeal is determined.

C. transfer $300 to the "Fee Account" and send Deft a $500 check on the "Clients' Fund Account."

D. send Deft a $500 check and leave $300 in the "Clients' Fund Account" until the matter is resolved with Deft.

Question 6.

Judge Alpha has been assigned to try a criminal prosecution by State against Deft. Ten years previously, Alpha, while serving as a deputy attorney general in State, initiated an investigation of Deft for suspected criminal conduct. The investigation did not establish any basis for prosecution. None of the matters previously investigated is involved in or affects the present prosecution.

Is it <u>proper</u> for Judge Alpha to try the case?

A. Yes, because none of the matters previously investigated is involved in or affects the present case.

B. Yes, unless Alpha might be prejudiced against Deft because of the prior investigation.

C. No, if Alpha had substantial responsibility in initiating the previous investigation of Deft.

D. No, if Alpha had substantial responsibility in determining that the previous investigation did not establish any basis for prosecution.

Question 7.

Attorney represented Landlord in a variety of matters over several years. Plaint, an elderly widow living on public assistance, filed suit against Landlord alleging that Landlord withheld without justification the security deposit on a rental unit that Plaint vacated three years ago. She brought the action for herself, without counsel, in small claims court. Attorney investigated the claim and learned that it was legally barred by the applicable statute of limitations, although Plaint's underlying claim was meritorious. Attorney told Landlord of the legal defense, but emphasized that Plaint's claim was just and that, in all fairness, the security deposit should be returned to Plaint. Attorney told Landlord:

> "I strongly recommend that you pay Plaint the full amount with interest. It is against your long-term business interests to be known in the community as a landlord who routinely withholds security deposits even though the tenant leaves the apartment in good condition. Paying the claim now will prevent future headaches for you."

Was Attorney's conduct <u>proper</u>?

A. Yes, if Landlord did not object to Attorney's advice and paid Plaint's claim.

B. Yes, because Attorney may refer to both legal and nonlegal considerations in advising a client.

C. No, unless Attorney's engagement letter informed Landlord that Attorney's advice on the matter would include both legal and nonlegal considerations.

D. No, because in advising Landlord to pay the full claim, Attorney failed to represent zealously Landlord's legal interests.

Question 8.

Attorney is a member of the bar and a salaried employee of the trust department of Bank. As part of his duties, he prepares a monthly newsletter concerning wills, trusts, estates, and taxes, which Bank sends to all of its customers. The newsletter contains a recommendation to the customer to review his or her will in light of the information contained and, if the customer has any questions, to bring the will to Bank's trust department where the trust officer will answer any questions without charge. The trust officer is not a lawyer. If the trust officer is unable to answer the customer's questions, the trust officer refers the customer to Attorney.

Is Attorney <u>subject to discipline</u> for the foregoing?

A. Yes, because Attorney is giving legal advice to persons who are not his clients.

B. Yes, because Attorney is aiding Bank in the unauthorized practice of law.

C. No, because no charge is made for Attorney's advice.

D. No, because Attorney is a member of the bar.

Question 9.

Alpha & Beta is a large firm that employs over 100 lawyers. Attorney Gamma was recently admitted to practice and was hired as a new associate of Alpha & Beta. Gamma was working late one night when he received a telephone call from his cousin Able. Able said that he was calling from the police station where he had just been arrested for possession of cocaine with intent to distribute. He was permitted to make only one phone call, and Gamma was the only lawyer he knew. Gamma responded that he had no criminal law experience and that Alpha & Beta did not handle criminal cases. Nevertheless, Able pleaded with Gamma to come to the police station and see what he could do to get Able out on bail. Gamma replied that he would do what he could.

Gamma went to the police station and using what information he recalled from his criminal law and procedure courses attempted to get Able released on bail. However, as a result of his inexperience, Gamma was unable to secure Able's release that night. The next morning, Gamma found an experienced criminal lawyer for Able, who obtained Able's release within one hour.

Was Gamma's conduct proper?

A. Yes, because neither referral nor consultation was practical under the circumstances.

B. Yes, because Gamma was a close relative of Able.

C. No, because Gamma had no special training or experience in criminal cases.

D. No, because Gamma did not have the requisite level of competence to accept representation in the case.

Question 10.

Attorney wants to make it easier for her clients to pay their bills for her fees.

Which of the following would be proper for Attorney?

I.   Accept bank credit cards in payment of Attorney's fees

II. Arrange for clients to obtain bank loans for the purpose of paying Attorney's fees

III. If a case is interesting, suggest that the client give Attorney publication rights concerning the case as partial payment of the fee

A. II only

B. I and II, but not III

C. I, II, and III

D. Neither I, nor II, nor III

Question 11.

Attorney practices law in a state that has experienced a business recession and where several banks have failed and others are severely pressed to preserve their solvency. Attorney maintains a Clients' Trust Account in Bank and that account is insured by the Federal Deposit Insurance Corporation against losses up to $100,000. Attorney also maintains his regular office account in the same bank and that account is insured to $100,000. During a particularly busy time, Attorney's bookkeeper told Attorney that the balance in the Clients' Trust Account had increased to $150,000. The bookkeeper noted that the office account had a balance of $30,000.

Which of the following courses of action by Attorney would be proper?

I.   Leave the Clients' Trust Account as is if the balance is likely to decrease to less than $100,000 within the next ten days.

II. Open another Clients' Trust Account in another bank and transfer some funds to the second Clients' Trust Account to maintain a fully insured balance in both accounts.

III. Temporarily transfer $50,000 from the Clients' Trust Account to the office account so the balance in both accounts is fully within insured limits.

A. I only

B. II only

C. I and II, but not III

D. II and III, but not I

Question 12.

Law Firm, a professional corporation with five lawyer shareholders, employs twenty-five additional lawyers.

Which of the following is(are) proper?

I. Employees who are members of the bar are not made shareholders until they have been with Law Firm ten years.

II. Manager, who is the office manager but not a member of the bar, is executive vice-president of Law Firm.

III. Widow, whose husband was a lawyer shareholder in Law Firm until his death two years ago, continues to hold husband's shares in Law Firm, distributed in his estate, until their child completes a law school education.

A. I only

B. I and II, but not III

C. I and III, but not II

D. I, II, and III

Question 13.

Attorney, who was recently admitted to the bar, has been appointed by the court as counsel for Deft, an indigent defendant charged with a felony. After consulting with Deft and attempting for two days to prepare the case for trial, Attorney became convinced that he lacked the knowledge and experience to represent Deft effectively.

Which of the following would be proper for Attorney?

I. Request permission of the court to withdraw from representing Deft because Attorney knows that he is not competent to handle the case

II. Request the court to appoint experienced co-counsel and grant a continuance to enable co-counsel to prepare the case

III. Explain the circumstances to Deft and, if Deft consents, proceed to represent Deft alone to the best of Attorney's ability

A. I only

B. I and II, but not III

C. II and III, but not I

D. I, II, and III

Question 14.

While an assistant district attorney, Attorney Alpha was in charge of the presentation before a grand jury of evidence that led to an indictment charging thirty-two defendants with conspiracy to sell controlled drugs. Shortly after the grand jury returned the indictments, Alpha resigned as assistant district attorney and became an associate in the law office of Attorney Beta, a sole practitioner. At the time of such association, Beta was the attorney for Deft, one of the indicted co-defendants.

Is it proper for Attorney Beta to continue to represent Deft?

A. Yes, if Alpha does not reveal to Beta any confidence or secret learned while an assistant district attorney.

B. Yes, because a public prosecutor must make timely disclosure to the defense attorney of any exculpatory evidence.

C. No, unless Alpha agrees not to participate in the representation of Deft.

D. No, because Alpha had substantial responsibility for the indictment of Deft.

Question 15.

Attorney filed an action on behalf of Client for breach of contract. In fact, Client had no legal basis for suit, but wanted to harass Defendant. In order to induce Attorney to file the action, Client made certain false statements of material fact to Attorney, which Attorney included in the complaint filed against Defendant.

At the trial of the case, Client took the stand and testified as set forth in the complaint. The trial court ordered judgment for Client. After entry of judgment, Client wrote Attorney a letter marked "Confidential," in which Client admitted that she had lied to Attorney and had testified falsely in the case.

Upon complaint of Defendant, who claimed Attorney had knowingly used false testimony in the case of Client v. Defendant, disciplinary proceedings were instituted against Attorney.

Is it proper for Attorney to use Client's letter to Attorney in Attorney's defense in the disciplinary proceedings?

A. Yes, if it is necessary to do so in order to protect Attorney's rights.

B. Yes, because Client had committed a fraud on the court in which the case was tried.

C. No, because Attorney learned the facts from Client in confidence.

D. No, if disclosure by Attorney could result in Client's prosecution for perjury.

Question 16.

Judge is presently serving on a state intermediate appellate court. This court, in opinions written by her, has decided several controversial cases in which the court has held that the Fourteenth Amendment to the United States Constitution does not guarantee due process protection to state prison inmates who are disciplined by prison authorities for violating the prison's rules of conduct. Judge is now a candidate for election to a vacancy on the state supreme court. She is vigorously opposed by several organizations concerned with the conditions under which prisoners are incarcerated in the state's prison. Judge is scheduled to be interviewed on television and has been informed that questions will be asked of her concerning those decisions and her attitude on the subject of prisoners' rights.

Which of the following is it proper for judge to say during the interview?

I. "I believe that the issues raised by the organizations opposing me are appropriate matters for legislative consideration."

II. "In my opinion, incarceration for the commission of a crime carries with it a loss of civil liberties in prison discipline proceedings."

III. "I am convinced I was right in those cases and will make the same decision in similar cases in the future."

A. I only

B. II only

C. I and II, but not III

D. I, II, and III

Questions 17 and 18 are based on the following fact situation: Attorney was formerly employed by Insurance Company as a lawyer solely to handle fire insurance claims. While so employed she investigated a fire loss claim of Claimant against Insurance Company. Attorney is now in private practice.

Question 17.

Assume the claim has not been settled and Claimant consults Attorney and asks Attorney either to represent him or refer him to another lawyer for suit on the claim.

Which of the following would be <u>proper</u> for Attorney to do?

I. Refuse to discuss the matter with Claimant

II. Represent Claimant

III. Refer Claimant to an associate in her law firm, provided Attorney does not share in any fee

IV. Give Claimant a list of lawyers who Attorney knows are competent and specialize in such claims

A. I only

B. I and II, but not III or IV

C. I and III, but not II or IV

D. I and IV, but not II or III

Question 18.

Assume that the original claim was settled. One year after Attorney left the employ of Insurance Company, Claimant slipped and fell in Insurance Company's office. Claimant now asks Attorney to represent him or refer him to another lawyer for suit on the "slip and fall" claim.

Which of the following would be <u>proper</u> for Attorney to do?

I. Refuse to discuss the matter with Claimant

II. Represent Claimant

III. Give Claimant a list of lawyers who Attorney knows are competent and specialize in such claims

A. I only

B. I and II, but not III

C. I and III, but not II

D. I, II, and III

Question 19.

Attorney prepared a will for Client and acted as one of the subscribing witnesses to Client's execution of the will. The will left all of Client's estate to Son, Client's son. Later, at Client's request, Attorney prepared a second will for Client and acted as one of the subscribing witnesses to Client's execution of the second will. The second will left one-half of Client's estate to Son and the other one-half to Housekeeper, Client's housekeeper. Client died and Housekeeper has offered the second will for probate.

If Son requests Attorney to represent him in opposing probate of the second will on the grounds of fraud and undue influence, is it proper for Attorney to do so?

A. Yes, because after Client's death Attorney may represent Son.

B. Yes, because Son is a beneficiary under both wills.

C. No, because an attorney guarantees the validity of a will that he or she prepares.

D. No, because Attorney would be taking a position adverse to a will she prepared and witnessed.

Question 20.

After both parties had completed the presentation of evidence and arguments, Judge took under advisement a case tried in Judge's court without a jury in which Attorney had represented Plaintiff. The case involved a difficult fact issue of causation and a difficult issue of law.

After the case was under advisement for several weeks, Attorney heard rumors that Judge was having difficulty determining the issue of factual causation and was uncertain about the applicable law. Immediately after hearing these rumors, Attorney telephoned Judge, told Judge of the rumors Attorney had heard, and asked if Judge would like to reopen the case for additional evidence and briefing from both parties. Thereafter Judge reopened the case for further testimony and requested supplementary briefs from both parties.

Was it proper for Attorney to communicate with Judge?

A. Yes, because both parties were given full opportunity to present their views on the issues in the case.

B. Yes, because Attorney did not make any suggestion as to how Judge should decide the matter.

C. No, because Attorney communicated with Judge on a pending matter without advising opposing counsel.

D. No, because Attorney caused Judge to reopen a case that had been taken under advisement.

Question 21.

Alpha represents Defendant in bitter and protracted litigation. Alpha, at Defendant's request, has made several offers of settlement to Plaintiff's lawyer Beta, all of which have been rejected.

During a week's recess in the trial, Alpha and Plaintiff were both present at a cocktail party. Plaintiff went over to Alpha and said: "Why can't we settle that case for $50,000? This trial is costing both sides more than it's worth."

Which of the following is a <u>proper</u> response by Alpha?

I.   "I can't discuss the matter with you."

II. "If that's the way you feel, why don't you and Defendant get together."

III. "I agree. We already have made several offers to settle this matter."

A. I only

B. I and II, but not III

C. II and III, but not I

D. I, II, and III

Question 22.

The law firm of Alpha and Beta has a radio commercial which states:

"Do you have a legal problem? Are you being sued? Consult Alpha and Beta, licensed attorneys at law. Initial conference charge is $25 for one hour. Act now and protect your interests. Call at 1234 Main Street; telephone area code (101) 123-4567."

Are Alpha and Beta <u>subject to discipline</u> for the commercial?

A. Yes, because the qualifications of the lawyers are not stated.

B. Yes, because the radio broadcast may encourage litigation.

C. No, if all the statements in the radio broadcast are true.

D. No, unless the radio broadcast is heard outside the state in which they are licensed.

Question 23.

Attorney, recently admitted to practice, opened an office near a residential neighborhood and published the following advertisement in the local newspaper.

COUPON

Get Acquainted With

Your Neighborhood Lawyer

A. Attorney

Suite 2 — 1100 Magnolia Avenue

Sunshine City, State 01000

Telephone: (555) 555-5555

In order to acquaint you with our services, we are offering a
one-hour consultation to review your estate plans, including
your wills, trusts, and similar documents, all at the nominal cost of
$25 to anyone presenting this coupon. Call now for an appointment.

Is Attorney subject to discipline?

A. Yes, because Attorney is soliciting business from persons with whom Attorney had no prior relationship.

B. Yes, because Attorney requires the use of a coupon.

C. No, if Attorney provides the services described for the fee stated.

D. No, unless Attorney is seeking business from persons who are already represented by a lawyer.

Question 24.

Attorney Alpha was retained by Client to incorporate Client's business, which previously had been operated as a sole proprietorship. Alpha noticed in Client's file copies of some correspondence from Client to Attorney Beta concerning the possibility of Beta's incorporating Client's business. Alpha questioned Client to make certain that any attorney-client relationship between Beta and Client had been terminated. Client told Alpha,

"It certainly has been terminated. When I discussed the matter with Beta six months ago, he asked for a retainer of $1,000, which I paid him. He did absolutely nothing after he got the money, even though I called him weekly, and finally, last week when I again complained, he returned the retainer. But don't say anything about it because Beta is an old friend of my family."

Is Alpha subject to discipline if she does not report her knowledge of Beta's conduct to the appropriate authority?

A. Yes, if Alpha believes Beta clearly was guilty of professional misconduct.

B. Yes, unless Alpha believes Beta does not usually neglect matters entrusted to him.

C. No, if Client was satisfied by Beta's return of the retainer.

D. No, unless Client agrees that Alpha may report the information.

Question 25.

Alpha & Beta, a general partnership, is a litigation firm practicing in State. It hires new law school graduates as associates. These new lawyers are largely left to their own resources to practice law. Alpha & Beta accepts many small litigation matters and assigns them to the associates for training purposes. No senior partners are assigned to supervise this work. It is assumed that if an associate needs help on a case, he or she will seek the guidance of a more senior attorney.

Client retained Alpha & Beta to pursue a claim for breach of contract against City. Associate, a first year associate, was assigned Client's case. Associate failed to comply with the applicable 30-day notice requirement for filing a complaint against City, and Client lost the chance to recover $5,000 owed to Client by City. When the complaint was dismissed for failure to comply with the notice requirement, Associate instead told Client that the case was dismissed on the merits.

Which of the following statements are correct?

I.   The law firm of Alpha & Beta is subject to discipline for failure to supervise Associate.

II. The individual partners of Alpha & Beta are subject to discipline for failure to make reasonable efforts to establish a system providing reasonable assurance that all lawyers in the firm comply with the rules of professional conduct.

III. Associate, an unsupervised subordinate lawyer, is subject to discipline for making misrepresentations to Client.

IV. Both the law firm of Alpha & Beta and Associate are subject to civil liability for Client's loss.

A. II and IV, but not I or III

B. I, III, and IV, but not II

C. II, III, and IV, but not I

D. I, II, III, and IV

Question 26.

Attorney, who represented Plaintiff, received a check from Deft payable to Attorney's order in the sum of $10,000 in settlement of Plaintiff's claim against Deft. Plaintiff had previously paid Attorney a fee so no part of the $10,000 was owed to Attorney.

Which of the following would be <u>proper</u>?

I.   Endorse the check and send it to Plaintiff

II. Deposit the check in Attorney's personal bank account and send Attorney's personal check for $10,000 to Plaintiff

III. Deposit the check in a Client Trust Account, advise Plaintiff, and forward a check drawn on that account to Plaintiff

A. I only

B. III only

C. I and III, but not II

D. I, II, and III

Question 27.

Attorney Alpha has tried many contested cases before Judge Gamma. Alpha believes the judge is lacking both in knowledge of the law and in good judgment and that Attorney Beta would make an excellent judge. Alpha wishes to defeat Judge Gamma and assist Beta in getting elected.

Alpha intends to contribute $5,000 to Beta's campaign. Is it <u>proper</u> for Alpha to do so?

A. Yes, Alpha may give $5,000 to Beta personally for his campaign.

B. Yes, if Alpha's contribution to Beta is made anonymously.

C. No, because Alpha is practicing before the court to which Beta seeks election.

D. No, unless Alpha gives the $5,000 to a committee formed to further Beta's election.

Question 28.

Attorney represented Seller in negotiating the sale of his ice cream parlor. Seller told Attorney in confidence that, although the business was once very profitable, recent profits have been stable but modest. As the negotiations proceeded, Buyer appeared to be losing interest in the deal. Hoping to restore Buyer's interest, Attorney stated, "The ice cream business is every American's dream: happy kids, steady profits, and a clear conscience." Buyer bought the ice cream parlor but was disappointed when his own profits proved to be modest.

Is Attorney <u>subject to discipline</u>?

A. Yes, because Attorney made a false statement of fact to Buyer.

B. Yes, because Attorney exaggerated the profitability of the business.

C. No, because Attorney represented Seller, not Buyer.

D. No, because Attorney's statement constitutes acceptable puffing in negotiations.

Question 29.

Attorney Alpha was retained by Passenger, a passenger on a bus, who had been injured in a collision between the bus and a truck. Passenger paid Alpha a retainer of $1,000 and agreed further that Alpha should have a fee of 25% of any recovery before filing suit, 30% of any recovery after suit was filed but before judgment, and 35% of any recovery after trial and judgment. Alpha promptly called the lawyer for the bus company and told him she was representing Passenger and would like to talk about a settlement. Alpha made an appointment to talk to the lawyer for the bus company but did not keep the appointment. Alpha continued to put off talking to the lawyer for the bus company. Meanwhile, Passenger became concerned because she had heard nothing from Alpha. Passenger called Alpha's office but was told Alpha was not in and would not call back. Passenger was told not to worry because Alpha would look after her interests. After ten months had passed, Passenger went to Attorney Beta for advice. Beta advised Passenger that the statute of limitations would run in one week and, with Passenger's consent, immediately filed suit for Passenger. Alpha, upon Passenger's demand, refunded the $1,000 Passenger had paid.

Is Alpha subject to discipline?

A. Yes, unless Alpha's time was completely occupied with work for other clients.

B. Yes, because Alpha neglected the representation of Passenger.

C. No, because Passenger's suit was filed before the statute of limitations ran.

D. No, because Alpha returned the $1,000 retainer to Passenger.

Question 30.

Attorney Alpha filed a personal injury suit on behalf of Plaintiff against Defendant. Defendant was personally served with process. Alpha knows that Defendant is insured by Insco and that Attorney Beta has been retained by Insco to represent Defendant. No responsive pleading has been filed on behalf of Defendant, and the time for filing expired over ten days ago.

Is Alpha subject to discipline if Alpha proceeds to have a default judgment entered?

A. Yes, because Alpha knew that Beta had been retained by Insco to represent Defendant.

B. Yes, because Alpha failed to extend professional courtesy to another lawyer.

C. No, because Alpha is properly representing her client's interests.

D. No, because any judgment will be satisfied by Insco.

Question 31.

Attorney is a candidate in a contested election for judicial office. Her opponent, Judge, is the incumbent and has occupied the bench for many years. The director of the state commission on judicial conduct, upon inquiry by Attorney, erroneously told Attorney that Judge had been reprimanded by the commission for misconduct in office. Attorney, who had confidence in the director, believed him. In fact, Judge had not been reprimanded by the commission; the commission had conducted hearings on Judge's alleged misconduct in office and, by a three to two vote, declined to reprimand Judge.

Decisions of the commission, including reprimands, are not confidential. Is Attorney subject to discipline for publicly stating that Judge had been reprimanded for misconduct?

A. Yes, because the official records of the commission would have disclosed the truth.

B. Yes, because Judge had not been reprimanded.

C. No, because Attorney reasonably relied on the director's information.

D. No, because Judge was a candidate in a contested election.

Question 32.

Attorney is a well-known, highly skilled litigator. Attorney's practice is in an area of law in which the trial proceedings are heard by the court without a jury.

In an interview with a prospective client, Attorney said, "I make certain that I give the campaign committee of every candidate for elective judicial office more money than any other lawyer gives, whether it's $500 or $5,000. Judges know who helps them get elected." The prospective client did not retain Attorney.

Is Attorney subject to discipline?

A. Yes, if Attorney's contributions are made without consideration of candidates' merits.

B. Yes, because Attorney implied that Attorney receives favored treatment by judges.

C. No, if Attorney's statements were true.

D. No, because the prospective client did not retain Attorney.

Question 33.

Judge is presiding in a case that has, as its main issue, a complicated point of commercial law. The lawyers have not presented the case to

Judge's satisfaction, and Judge believes she needs additional legal advice. Judge's former partner in law practice, Attorney, is an expert in the field of law that is at issue. Attorney has no interest in the case.

Is it <u>proper</u> for Judge to consult Attorney?

A. Yes, because Attorney has no interest in the case.

B. Yes, if Judge believes that Attorney's advice is needed to serve the interests of justice.

C. No, unless all parties in the case first give their written consent to Judge's consultation with Attorney.

D. No, unless Judge informs the parties of Attorney's identity and the substance of Attorney's advice, and asks for their responses.

Question 34.

Attorney's advertisement in the local newspaper includes the following information, all of which is true:

I.   Attorney, BA., magna cum laude, Eastern College; J.D., summa cum laude, State Law School; LL.M., Eastern Law School.

II.   My offices are open Monday through Friday from 9:00 a.m. to 5:00 p.m., but you may call my answering service twenty-four hours a day, seven days a week.

III. I speak Modern Greek fluently.

For which, if any, of these statements is Attorney <u>subject to discipline</u>?

A. III only

B. I and II, but not III

C. I, II, and III

D. Neither I, nor II, nor III

Question 35.

Trustco, a trust company, entered into the following arrangement with Attorney, a lawyer newly admitted to the bar.

Trustco would provide Attorney with free office space in the building in which Trustco had its offices. If a customer of Trustco contacted Trustco about a trust or will, an officer of Trustco, who is not a lawyer, would advise the customer and help the customer work out the details of the trust or will. The customer would be informed that the necessary documents would be prepared by Trustco's staff. The completed documents would be submitted by an officer of Trustco to the customer for execution.

Attorney, in accordance with a memorandum from Trustco's trust officer detailing the plan, would prepare the necessary documents. Attorney would never meet with the customer and would not charge the customer for these services. Attorney would be free to engage in private practice, subject only to the limitation that Attorney could not accept employment adverse to Trustco.

Is Attorney <u>subject to discipline</u> for entering into the arrangement with Trustco?

A. Yes, because Attorney is restricting his right to practice.

B. Yes, because Attorney is aiding Trustco in the practice of law.

C. No, because Attorney is not charging the customer for his services.

D. No, because Attorney is not giving advice to Trustco's customers.

Question 36.

Attorney represented Husband and Wife in the purchase of a business financed by contributions from their respective separate funds. The business was jointly operated by Husband and Wife after acquisition. After several years, a dispute arose over the management of the business. Husband and Wife sought Attorney's advice, and the matter was settled on the basis of an agreement drawn by Attorney and signed by Husband and Wife. Later, Wife asked Attorney to represent her in litigation against Husband based on the claim that Husband was guilty of fraud and misrepresentation in the negotiations for the prior settlement agreement.

Is it <u>proper</u> for Attorney to represent Wife in this matter?

A. Yes, if all information relevant to the litigation was received by Attorney in the presence of both Husband and Wife.

B. Yes, if there is reason to believe Husband misled both Wife and Attorney at the time of the prior agreement.

C. No, because Attorney had previously acted for both parties in reaching the agreement now in dispute.

D. No, unless Husband is now represented by independent counsel.

Question 37.

Alpha and Beta are members of the bar in the same community but have never practiced together. Beta is a candidate in a contested election for judicial office. Beta is opposed by Delta, another lawyer in the community. Alpha believes Beta is better qualified than Delta for the judiciary and is supporting Beta's candidacy.

Which of the following would be proper for Alpha?

I.   Solicit public endorsements for Beta's candidacy by other attorneys in the community who know Beta and are likely to appear before Beta if Beta becomes a judge.

II. Solicit contributions to Beta's campaign committee from other attorneys in the community who are likely to appear before Beta if Beta becomes a judge.

III. Publicly oppose the candidacy of Delta.

A. I only

B. I and II, but not III

C. I and III, but not II

D. I, II, and III

Question 38.

Attorney advertises on the local television station. In the advertisements, a professional actor says:

"Do you need a lawyer? Call Attorney—her telephone number is area code 555-555-5555. Her fees might be lower than you think."

Attorney approved the prerecorded advertisement and is keeping in her office files a copy of the recording of the actual transmission and a record of when each transmission was made.

Is the advertisement proper?

A. Yes.

B. No, unless Attorney's fees are lower than those generally charged in the area where she practices.

C. No, because she used a professional actor for the television advertisement.

D. No, if she makes a charge for the initial consultation.

Questions **39** and **40** are based on the following fact situation. Deft, who has been indicted for auto theft, is represented by Attorney. Prosecutor reasonably believes that Deft committed the offense, but, because of Deft's youth, it is in the interest of justice to permit Deft to plead guilty to the lesser offense of "joy-riding" in return for an agreement by Prosecutor to recommend probation. Prosecutor has so advised Attorney, but Attorney told Prosecutor she would not plea bargain and would insist on a jury trial. Attorney informed Deft of Prosecutor's offer and advised Deft not to accept it. Deft followed Attorney's advice. Attorney is a candidate for public office, and Prosecutor suspects that Attorney is insisting on a trial of the case to secure publicity for herself.

Question 39.

Which of the following would be proper for Prosecutor?

I.   Send a member of his staff who is not a lawyer to consult with Deft.

II. Move the trial court to dismiss the indictment and accept a new complaint charging the offense of "joy-riding."

III. Proceed to trial on the indictment and prosecute the case vigorously.

A. II only

B. III only

C. I and II, but not III

D. II and III, but not I

Question 40.

Assume for the purposes of this question ONLY that Deft was tried, convicted, and sentenced to prison for two years.

Must Prosecutor report to the disciplinary authority his suspicions about Attorney's conduct of the case?

A. Yes, because Deft suffered a detriment from Attorney's refusal to plea bargain.

B. Yes, if Attorney in fact received widespread publicity as a result of the trial.

C. No, unless Prosecutor has knowledge that Attorney's refusal to plea bargain was due to personal motives.

D. No, if Attorney zealously and competently represented Deft at the trial.

Question 41.

Driver consulted Attorney and asked Attorney to represent Driver, who was being prosecuted for driving while intoxicated in a jurisdiction in which there is an increased penalty for a second offense. Driver told Attorney that his driver's license had been obtained under an assumed name because his prior license had been suspended for driving while under the influence of alcohol. Driver asked Attorney not to disclose Driver's true name during the course of the representation and told Attorney that, if called as a witness, he would give his assumed name. Attorney informed Driver that, in order properly to defend the case, Attorney must call Driver as a witness.

Attorney called Driver as a witness and, in response to Attorney's question "what is your name?", Driver gave his assumed name and not his true name.

Is Attorney subject to discipline?

A. Yes, because Attorney knowingly used false testimony.

B. Yes, if Driver committed a felony when he obtained the driver's license under an assumed name.

C. No, because Attorney's knowledge of Driver's true name was obtained during the course of representation.

D. No, unless Drivers true name is an issue in the proceeding.

Question 42.

Attorney represents Client, a plaintiff in a personal injury action. Wit was an eyewitness to the accident. Wit lives about 500 miles distant from the city where the case will be tried. Attorney interviewed Wit and determined that Wit's testimony would be favorable for Client. Wit asked Attorney to pay Wit, in addition to the statutory witness fees while attending the trial, the following:

I.   Reimbursement for actual travel expenses while attending the trial.

II. Reimbursement for lost wages while present at the trial.

III. An amount equal to 5% of any recovery in the matter.

If Attorney agrees to pay Wit the above, for which, if any, is Attorney subject to discipline?

A. III only

B. II and III, but not I

C. I, II, and III

D. Neither I, nor II, nor III

Question 43.

Judge is a judge of the trial court in City. Judge has served for many years as a director of a charitable organization that maintains a camp for disadvantaged children. The organization has never been involved in litigation. Judge has not received any compensation for her services. The charity has decided to sponsor a public testimonial dinner in Judge's honor. As part of the occasion, the local bar association intends to commission and present to Judge her portrait at a cost of $4,000.

The money to pay for the portrait will come from a "public testimonial fund" that will be raised by the City Bar Association from contributions of lawyers who are members of the association and who practice in the courts of City.

Is it proper for Judge to accept the gift of the portrait?

A. Yes, because the gift is incident to a public testimonial for Judge.

B. Yes, because Judge did not receive compensation for her services to the charitable organization.

C. No, because the cost of the gift exceeds $1,000.

D. No, because the funds for the gift are contributed by lawyers who practice in the courts of City.

Question 44.

Attorney, who had represented Testator for many years, prepared Testator's will and acted as one of the two subscribing witnesses to its execution. The will gave 10% of Testator's estate to Testator's housekeeper, 10% to Testator's son and sole heir, Son, and the residue to charity. Upon Testator's death one year later, Executor, the executor named in the will, asked Attorney to represent him in probating the will and administering the estate. At that time Executor informed

Attorney that Son had notified him that he would contest the probate of the will on the grounds that Testator lacked the required mental capacity at the time the will was executed. Attorney believes that Testator was fully competent at all times and will so testify, if called as a witness. The other subscribing witness to Testator's will predeceased Testator.

Is it proper for Attorney to represent Executor in the probate of the will?

A. Yes, because Attorney is the sole surviving witness to the execution of the will.

B. Yes, because Attorney's testimony will support the validity of the will.

C. No, because Attorney will be called to testify on a contested issue of fact.

D. No, because Attorney will be representing an interest adverse to Testator's heir at law.

Question 45.

Attorney represented Buyer in a real estate transaction. Due to Attorney's negligence in drafting the purchase agreement. Buyer was required to pay for a survey that should have been paid by Seller, the other party to the transaction. Attorney fully disclosed this negligence to Buyer, and Buyer suggested that he would be satisfied If Attorney simply reimbursed Buyer for the entire cost of the survey.

Although Buyer might have recovered additional damages if a malpractice action were filed, Attorney reasonably believed that the proposed settlement was fair to Buyer. Accordingly, in order to forestall a malpractice action, Attorney readily agreed to make the reimbursement. Attorney drafted a settlement agreement, and it was executed by both Attorney and Buyer.

Was Attorney's conduct proper?

A. Yes, if Attorney advised Buyer in writing that Buyer should seek independent representation before deciding to enter into the settlement agreement.

B. Yes, because Attorney reasonably believed that the proposed settlement was fair to Buyer.

C. No, because Attorney settled a case involving liability for malpractice while the matter was still ongoing.

D. No, unless Buyer was separately represented in negotiating and finalizing the settlement agreement.

Question 46.

Attorney Alpha, a member of the bar, placed a printed flyer in the booth of each artist exhibiting works at a county fair. The face of the flyer contained the following information:

"I, Alpha, am an attorney, with offices in 800 Bank Building, telephone (555) 555-5555. I have a J.D. degree from State Law School and an M.A. degree in fine arts from State University. My practice includes representing artists in negotiating contracts between artists and dealers and protecting artists' interests. You can find me in the van parked at the fair entrance."

All factual information on the face of the flyer was correct. There was a retainer agreement on the back of the flyer. At the entrance to the fair, Alpha parked a van with a sign that read "Alpha-Attorney at Law."

For which, if any, of the following is Alpha <u>subject to discipline</u>?

I.   Placing copies of the flyer in the booth of each artist

II. Including a retainer agreement on the back of the flyer

III. Parking the van with the sign on it at the fair entrance

A. III only

B. I and II, but not III

C. I, II, and III

D. Neither I, nor II, nor III

Question 47.

Witness was subpoenaed to appear and testify at a state legislative committee hearing. Witness retained Attorney to represent her at the hearing. During the hearing, Attorney, reasonably believing that it was in Witness's best interest not to answer, advised Witness not to answer certain questions on the grounds that Witness had a constitutional right not to answer. The committee chairperson directed Witness to answer and cautioned her that refusal to answer was a misdemeanor and that criminal prosecution would be instituted if she did not answer.

Upon Attorney's advice, Witness persisted in her refusal to answer. Witness was subsequently convicted for her refusal to answer.

Is Attorney subject to discipline?

A. Yes, because his advice to Witness was not legally sound.

B. Yes, because Witness, in acting on Attorney's advice, committed a crime.

C. No, if the offense Witness committed did not involve moral turpitude.

D. No, if Attorney reasonably believed Witness had a legal right to refuse to answer the questions.

Question 48.

Attorney represented Client on a minor personal injury claim against Driver, an uninsured motorist. Attorney represented Client on a 30% contingent fee basis. Pursuant to a negotiated settlement in the amount of $2,000, Driver agreed to send Attorney a $100 check, made payable to Attorney, in each of the ensuing twenty months.

Which of the following dispositions of each monthly check would be proper for Attorney?

I.   Deposit the check into her office account and immediately write Client a check for $70 from that account.

II.   Deposit the check into a separate account established for Client and immediately request Client to pay Attorney $30.

III. Deposit the check into a trust account in which funds belonging to all Attorney's clients are deposited and immediately write Client a check for $70 and herself a check for $30 from that account.

A. II only

B. III only

C. I and II, but not III

D. II and III, but not I

Question 49.

Attorney Alpha currently represents Builder, a building contractor and the plaintiff in a suit to recover for breach of a contract to build a house. Builder also has pending before the zoning commission a petition to rezone property Builder owns. Builder is represented by Attorney Beta in the zoning matter.

Neighbor, who owns property adjoining that of Builder, has asked Alpha to represent Neighbor in opposing Builder's petition for rezoning. Neighbor knows that Alpha represents Builder in the contract action.

Is it <u>proper</u> for Alpha to represent Neighbor in the zoning matter?

A. Yes, if there is no common issue of law or fact between the two matters.

B. Yes, because one matter is a judicial proceeding and the other is an administrative proceeding.

C. No, because Alpha is currently representing Builder in the contract action.

D. No, if there is a possibility that both matters will be appealed to the same court.

Question 50.

Pros, an elected prosecutor in City, plans to run for relection in six months. Last year two teenage girls were kidnapped from a shopping center and sexually assaulted. The community was in an uproar about the crime and put pressure on Pros to indict and convict the assailant. Four months ago, Deft was arrested and charged with the crimes. The trial is scheduled to begin next week.

Pros met with the police chief last week to review the evidence in the case. At that time, Pros first learned that, before they were interviewed by the detective in charge of sexual assault crimes, the two victims had been tape-recorded discussing the case between themselves in an interview room. Reviewing the tape, Pros realized that the girls' descriptions of the assailant differed significantly in terms of height, weight and hair color. When officially interviewed, however, their descriptions matched almost perfectly.

Deft's appointed counsel was busy handling a large caseload of indigent defendants and neglected to seek access to the prosecution's investigative file. Pros was virtually certain that Deft's counsel was unaware of the tape recording. Given the other evidence in the case, Pros reasonably believed that the girls accurately identified Deft as their assailant. Pros did not reveal the existence of the tape to defense counsel.

Is Pros subject to discipline?

A. Yes, because the tape raises a legitimate question about the victims' eyewitness identification of Deft as the assailant.

B. Yes, unless Pros reasonably believed that the girls accurately identified Deft as their assailant.

C. No, because under the adversary system of criminal justice, it is expected that each party will marshal the evidence best supporting its own position.

D. No, unless Deft's counsel submitted a request for all mitigating or exculpatory evidence before the start of trial.

B. Author's Answers to Model Questions

Question 1.

B is the correct answer. A lawyer must provide competent representation to clients, Model Rule 1.1, which requires having the legal knowledge and skill necessary for the representation. In order to maintain the required level of knowledge and skill, a lawyer should keep abreast of changes in the law through continuing study and education, as well as comply with any continuing education requirements to which the lawyer is subject. Model Rule 1.1, Comment [6]. Even though Gamma is not required to attend continuing legal education courses because State does not require lawyers to participate in continuing legal education, he is not relieved of his duty to maintain competence, which he can do through independent study.

A is incorrect. Gamma must maintain competence without regard to the cost of doing so.

C is incorrect. Obviously continuing education courses are not the only means by which Gamma can maintain competence.

D is incorrect. Being insured against malpractice has nothing to do with a lawyer's duty to maintain the legal knowledge and skills needed to provide competent representation.

Question 2.

A is the correct answer. It relies only on the option in III. The controlling Rule is Model Rule 8.1, which deals with a lawyer's duty in connection with a bar applicant. The Rule means that a lawyer submitting a letter recommending a bar applicant must rely upon his own knowledge about the applicant. He may not rely on information supplied by someone else. Thus, a lawyer must not knowingly make a false statement of material fact, or knowingly fail to respond to a lawful demand for information by an admissions authority in connection with a bar admission application. The purpose of the Rule is to help in maintaining the integrity of the bar by identifying those who are unfit for admission.

B is incorrect because it relies on and I and II and excludes III. A lawyer may not rely on someone else's assurances in writing a letter of recommendation (I) even if the lawyer himself has no unfavorable information (II).

C is incorrect because it relies in part on I, which is incorrect.

D is incorrect because it relies in part on I and II, both of which are incorrect.

Question 3.

A is the correct answer. Model Rule 8.4 defines the acts that constitute misconduct by a lawyer. Model Rule 8.4(c) describes as professional misconduct any conduct "involving dishonesty, fraud, deceit or misrepresentation." The definition is not limited to misconduct in connection with the practice of law but, under Comment [2], extends to all offenses that "indicate lack of those characteristics relevant to law practice," including violence, dishonesty and breach of trust. Also, misconduct is misconduct wherever it occurs — whether in the state in which the attorney is licensed to practice or elsewhere. Here, Alpha has knowingly filed a false financial statement in connection with a professional license application, a clear violation of the Rule.

B is incorrect. The definition of misconduct extends far beyond conviction for a criminal offense. Comment [2] to Model Rule 8.4 states, "Many kinds of illegal conduct reflect adversely on fitness to practice law such as offenses involving fraud and the offense of willful failure to file an income tax return."

C is incorrect. A lawyer is judged not only by his conduct in his capacity as lawyer but all conduct that measures his honesty, trustworthiness and general fitness as a lawyer. See Model Rule 8.4(b).

D is incorrect. Geography has nothing to do with the concept of misconduct. Misconduct is misconduct wherever it occurs.

Question 4.

D is the correct answer. Lawyers are prohibited from soliciting business from prospective clients by in-person contact or live telephone contact. Model Rule 7.3. The key word is prospective — i.e., "future." The prohibition against solicitation does not extend to persons with whom the lawyer has had a prior personal or professional relationship, "or where the lawyer is motivated by considerations other than the lawyer's pecuniary gain." Hence, the prohibition does not extend to contacts with former clients, personal friends or family members. On these facts, Attorney is dealing with a former client whose interests may be adversely affected if Attorney does not advise her of the new IRS regulation. We are entitled to assume that Attorney was motivated not by a desire for pecuniary gain but by a good-faith instinct to help a former client. In any event, it's enough that Testatrix is a former client.

A is incorrect. Attorney is permitted to contact Testatrix as a former client whether or not she has reason to believe Testatrix has another attorney. Attorney has no way of knowing whether Testatrix has another attorney of if the other attorney is a specialist in tax law or is even aware of the new regulation. The Rule does not require the attorney to inquire into these facts.

B is incorrect. The test is not whether the person is a current client but whether the person is a former client. For purposes of Model Rule 7.3, once a client always a client.

C is incorrect. Attorney is free to offer and supply her services to Testatrix in any way Testatrix may be willing to utilize them. The issue here is in-person solicitation, not limits on the scope of representation.

Question 5.

D is the correct answer. The answer recognizes the three basic principles a lawyer must observe when dealing with client funds: (1) client funds must always be kept separate from the lawyer's funds in a designated clients' escrow account; (2) as soon as the client's interest in the funds is fixed, the client's money must be delivered to the client; and (3) if both the client and the attorney claim any interest in any part of the funds — e.g., if a dispute arises as to the lawyer's fees — the funds must remain in the separate client account until there is an accounting and their respective interests can be severed — e.g., the dispute is resolved. Model Rule 1.15. Here, attorney's maximum claim was for fees totaling 6 hours × $50 = $300. When the bail hearing was completed, client's interest in the advance was $500. Attorney had a duty to return this promptly. Because the client had demanded $800, the lawyer's fee of $300 was in dispute. The money representing the fee had to be retained in the Clients' Fund Account until the dispute was resolved.

A is incorrect. The funds in dispute totaled only $300. The balance of $500 was not in dispute and belonged to the client when it was not applied to the bail costs. Attorney was under a duty to return $500 to the client because the money was not used for the purpose intended.

B is incorrect. Because the fee of $300 was in dispute, Attorney had no right to transfer that sum to his fee account. He was required to retain the funds in his Clients' Fund Account until the dispute was resolved. Further, Attorney had no right to retain the balance of $500 in either account pending the appeal. The money was deposited with Attorney only in connection with the bail application, not the appeal itself.

C is incorrect. Attorney was right to send the $500 to the client but wrong in transferring $300 to his fee account. So long as his fee was in dispute, the $300 had to be retained in the Clients' Fund Account. Model Rule 1.15(e).

Question 6.

B is the correct answer. A judge is expected to perform his duties fairly, impartially and without prejudice against any litigant. CJC, Canon 3, (E). The test is the judge's mindset as perceived by a reasonable observer. If the judge has a personal bias towards a party or his lawyer, or personal knowledge of disputed evidentiary facts concerning the proceeding, he must disqualify himself. Also, if he or a former law partner has served either side as a lawyer concerning the matter, or if he has served as a material witness in the matter, he must disqualify himself. B correctly states the issue facing Judge Alpha. If there is any chance that his prior investigation of Deft will prejudice his judgment, he must disqualify himself.

A is incorrect because it misstates the test for disqualification. It doesn't matter that the prior investigation is unrelated to the present case. If, in fact, Judge Alpha is adversely influenced by his participation in the investigation, he must disqualify himself.

C is incorrect. Although it states a basis for suspecting prejudice by Judge Alpha against Deft, it is not as good an answer as B, which correctly frames the issue as one of potential prejudice.

D is incorrect. This option does not revolve around Judge Alpha's state of mind. It is just as reasonable to conclude that Judge Alpha was not prejudiced by the prior investigation as that he was prejudiced. The issue is whether he was and is actually prejudiced against Deft. B is the best formula for disposing of that issue.

Question 7.

B is the correct answer. When a lawyer gives a client advice, she may rely on considerations other than those involved in giving purely technical legal advice. Model Rule 2.1. She should exercise her professional judgment and give candid advice. It is proper for her to rely on moral, economic, and social factors in doing so, which is what Attorney did here.

A is incorrect because the issue isn't whether Landlord accepted Attorney's advice — and in fact a lawyer should not be deterred from giving candid advice simply because the client might find it unpalatable — but whether Attorney acted properly in going beyond the technical legal aspect of the case in advising Landlord.

C is incorrect. An initial, or engagement, letter to the client is concerned with fees. It's purpose is to make clear what services the lawyer will provide and what she will charge for them, not in what form she will render advice. Model Rule 1.5.

D is incorrect. It raises the issue of a lawyer's responsibility to "act with ...zeal in advocacy." Model Rule 1.3, Comment [1]. But that isn't really the issue here. The issue is what is the proper scope for the advice a lawyer gives a client. Not only is it proper for a lawyer to refer to considerations other than the law in advising a client, she also has a responsibility to exercise independent professional judgment in advising a client and to advise the client in a straightforward, honest manner, in the best interests of the client. Attorney has done exactly that.

Question 8.

B is the correct answer. Basic to the integrity of the legal profession is the principle that only persons admitted to practice may engage in practice. Any person who is not a lawyer but who gives legal advice is said to engage in the unauthorized practice of law. Any lawyer who helps a non-lawyer to engage in the unauthorized practice of law violates Model Rule 5.5(a). Here, Attorney is helping the bank to encourage its customers to review their wills with trusts officers who are not lawyers. The preparation, drafting, interpretation, and amendment of wills and trust documents are functions that fall within the definition of legal services.

A is incorrect. A lawyer is not prevented from giving advice to a non-client. When the interests of a client may be involved, however, the lawyer is required to avoid stating or implying to the non-client that the lawyer is disinterested. If the lawyer knows or reasonably should know that the unrepresented person misunderstands his role in the matter, he must make reasonable efforts to correct the misunderstanding. Model Rule 4.3.

C is incorrect. Whether Attorney charges a fee or not, he's part of a scheme which enables the bank's trust officers to give legal advice.

D is incorrect. The very nub of Attorney's violation is that he is a member of the bar. Because he is, he is enjoined from assisting the bank to engage in the practice of law.

Question 9.

A is the correct answer. Although Gamma does not have the "requisite knowledge and skill" to competently represent Able and knows he doesn't, this scenario would fall under the "emergency" situation discussed in Model Rule 1.1, Comment [3]. It would have been impractical for Gamma to refer Alpha to another lawyer or to consult with another lawyer, so he therefore gave reasonably necessary assistance to get Alpha out on bail.

B is incorrect. That Gamma and Able are relatives has nothing to do with whether Gamma can represent Able competently. Gamma must decide whether he has the requisite knowledge and skill to provide Able with competent representation regardless of their relationship.

C is incorrect. It is precisely because of Gamma's inexperience that he made the decision that he did. He acted appropriately in giving assistance in an "emergency" situation, which included finding an experienced criminal lawyer for Able.

D is incorrect. Gamma did not accept representation.

Question 10.

B is the correct answer. This answer recognizes that Choices I and II are correct but that Choice III is not correct. Model Rule 1.5 deals with the subject of fees. The key requirement of the Rule is that fees shall be reasonable. There is no provision in the Rule which specifies the manner of payment. A client may pay by any device accepted in ordinary commerce — i.e., cash, check, promissory note, bank credit card, etc. Recently, lawyers have even accepted equity interests in the client as payment. Also, there is nothing to prevent a lawyer from helping his client to arrange a bank loan for any legitimate purpose, including payment of the lawyer's fees. Model Rule 1.8(e) instructs a lawyer "not to provide financial assistance to a client in connection with pending or contemplated litigation" (except for advances of court costs and litigation expenses), but helping to arrange a bank loan would not appear to fall within the prohibition, although a direct loan from the lawyer to the client would.

A is incorrect because it relies only on Choice II. Choice I is also correct.

C is incorrect because it includes Choice III. Choice III describes a transaction between lawyer and client which is prohibited under Model Rule 1.8(d). The Rule directs a lawyer not to make an agreement giving the lawyer any "literary or media rights" based in substantial part on information relating to the representation, before the conclusion of the representation. The Rule prevents conflicts of interest that may prompt a lawyer to be more concerned about his own economic interests than the client's welfare.

Question 11.

B is the correct answer. Only II complies with Model Rule 1.15, which requires that a lawyer hold property of others with the care required of a professional fiduciary *and* keep client funds separate from the lawyer's funds.

A is incorrect because it relies on I, and gambling that the balance of the Trust account will decrease in 10 days to the insured amount is unacceptable behavior in a fiduciary.

C is incorrect because it relies in part on I.

D is incorrect because it relies on III, and a lawyer may deposit the lawyer's own funds in a client trust account only for the purpose of paying bank service charges and only in the amount necessary for that purpose. Model Rule 1.15(b).

Question 12.

A is the correct answer. The only correct option of the three given is option I. A law firm may govern the terms under which associates who are lawyers advance through the firm to achieve partnership or (in the case of professional corporations) shareholder status. The shareholders or partners may do this by agreement. The controlling Rule is Model Rule 5.4, which enunciates the very basic principles that lawyers may not share fees with non-lawyers and that non-lawyers may not control the professional judgment of a lawyer.

B is incorrect because it incorporates option II. Model Rule 5.4(d)(2) says very simply: "A lawyer shall not practice with or in the form of a professional corporation or association authorized to practice law for a profit, if. . .a non-lawyer is a corporate director or officer thereof; . . ."

C is incorrect because it depends in part on option III. Because Widow is presumably a non-lawyer, she may not continue indefinitely to act as shareholder and therefore share in the firm's fees, no matter how worthy the purpose. Model Rule 5.4(a)(1) permits the payment of money to a decedent's widow or estate only for "a reasonable period of time after the lawyer's death."

D is incorrect because it depends on all three options, two of which are wrong, as we have seen.

Question 13.

B is the correct answer because it recognizes that both I and II are proper options. The most basic rule in the litany of disciplinary rules is the very first rule, Model Rule 1.1, which requires a lawyer to "provide competent representation to a client." Competent representation is defined as "the legal knowledge, skill, thoroughness and preparation reasonably necessary for the representation." In a criminal case, the consequence of incompetent representation is especially grave, and a lawyer is well-advised to reflect carefully about his knowledge and skill before proceeding to trial. A lawyer who feels himself inadequate to offer competent representation in a criminal case has two options — he may ask the court for leave to withdraw or he may ask for appointment of more experienced co-counsel. The latter is usually the better course, because it enables the inexperienced lawyer to participate and learn and because it upsets the court's routine less, and protects the client more, than withdrawal. A young and/or experienced lawyer is also well-advised to seek the court's help very soon after he takes on the representation. First of all, a criminal defendant's rights can be jeopardized in the first hours after the appointment, and, also, the courts do not look kindly on a lawyer who asks to withdraw or to have other counsel appointed on the eve of trial.

A is incorrect because it adopts only option I. Option II also represents proper conduct under the facts.

C is incorrect. It omits option I, which is correct. Although it adopts option II, it also adopts option III, which is wrong. A lawyer may not transfer the test of his competence to the client by asking for the client's consent. The basis for this rule is obvious. The client has no knowledge upon which to base a judgment on the lawyer's competence. Only the lawyer knows whether he has the knowledge, skill and experience to represent the client competently.

D is incorrect because it includes option III, which is wrong.

Question 14.

D is the correct answer. These facts invoke the concepts of conflicts of interest and imputed disqualification. Model Rule 1.9 deals with the conflict faced by a lawyer who has represented one client, terminates the representation, and then is asked to represent a new client with interests adverse to those of the lawyer's former client. If we simplify these facts, it's clear that Attorney Alpha could not himself represent Deft after he participated in the investigation of Deft because the interests of Deft are adverse to the district attorney's interests. Model Rule 1.9(a). But the question asks about Beta's representation of Deft, not

Alpha's. Model Rule 1.10 extends Alpha's disqualification to Beta under the imputed disqualification rule; "While lawyers are associated in a firm, none of them shall knowingly represent a client when any one of them practicing alone would be prohibited from doing so by Model Rules 1.7. or 1.9."

A is incorrect. Model Rule 1.9 doesn't give the lawyer with the prohibited conflict the discretion to decide that he can protect the interests of the new client by protecting confidences. So long as either: (1) the lawyer himself formerly represented a client in a substantially related matter with interests adverse to the new client's interests (Model Rule 1.9 (a)): or (2) the lawyer was associated with a firm representing a client with interests adverse to his present client about whom the lawyer acquired information protected by the confidentiality rules which is material to the matter (Model Rule 1.9(b)), the lawyer may not represent the new client.

B is incorrect. It states correctly a basic rule that prosecutors must follow, but it is not responsive to the question. The facts do not suggest that there was any exculpatory evidence or that Alpha knew of or withheld any. Also, the statement in B is irrelevant to the facts because Alpha is no longer a prosecutor.

C is incorrect. The initial prohibition is directed at Alpha because he's the lawyer with the conflict between former and present client. But the prohibition extends to Beta under the imputed disqualification rule, whether or not Alpha participates. Model Rule 1.10.

Question 15.

A is the correct answer. The question deals with the general obligation of a lawyer not to reveal any information relating to representation of a client without the client's consent after consultation. The obligation is defined in Model Rule 1.6(a). Model Rule 1.6(b) creates three exceptions to the general rule. The first exception permits a lawyer to reveal a client confidence to prevent reasonably certain death or substantial bodily harm. The second exception permits a lawyer to reveal a client confidence to secure legal advice about his or her compliance with the Rules. The third exception permits a lawyer to reveal a client confidence in order to defend himself in a controversy with the client, to defend himself against a criminal charge or civil claim for conduct involving the client, or to respond to allegations in any proceeding concerning the representation. Because Defendant has made a serious charge which would have grave consequences for Attorney if accepted as true, Attorney has a right to reveal the contents of Client's letter.

B is incorrect. Although Client has indeed committed a fraud on the court, Attorney would be obligated not to reveal the fraud except for the need to protect himself against the false accusation of complicity. Client fraud does not fall within one of the two exceptions to the general duty of confidentiality.

C is incorrect. Whether or not Attorney learned the facts in confidences, he has a right to disclose them in order to protect himself in the disciplinary proceeding.

D is incorrect. When a lawyer is accused of a disciplinary infraction, he has a right to disclose a client's confidences to defend himself. In the balance between the lawyer's right to defend himself and the consequences to the client of revealing the client's confidence, the Rules have tipped the scales in favor of the lawyer, whose livelihood and reputation are at stake. Otherwise, the lawyer would be unable to defend himself.

Question 16.

A is the correct answer. Under the facts, Judge is again a candidate for judicial office. In her prior opinions, she has taken a consistent position which has precipitated a political response that is apparently central to the election. Her conduct as candidate for election is controlled by the Code of Judicial Conduct, Canon 5(A)(3). Canon 5(A)(3)(d) states: "A candidate for a judicial office...shall not...(ii) with respect to cases, controversies or issues that are likely to come before the court make pledges, promises or commitments that are inconsistent with the impartial performance of the adjudicative duties of the office." Clearly, an issue that has already come before the court several times, especially one exciting such controversy, is likely to come before the court again. Judge would be precluded from making any statement that would appear to commit her to a particular position on subsequent cases, especially a position she has announced before. Judges are supposed to rule on the basis of the evidence and the law of the case immediately before them, not according to some personal prejudice. Option I is the only option which correctly recites a statement Judge is permitted to make. It does not commit her in her role as judge and is only a nonbinding recommendation to the legislature.

B is incorrect. It relies on option II, which is clearly a commitment to decide future cases before the court in exactly the same way as prior cases, without reference to changing circumstances or specific evidence.

C is incorrect. It relies in Part on option II, which is wrong.

D is incorrect. It relies on options II and III. We have seen that option II is wrong. Option III is the worst kind of statement a judge can make. It reflects a complete rejection of the first principle of judging: the obligation to act with integrity and impartiality. No one can act as judge who is unable to respond fairly and without bias to the litigants before him. Judge has committed herself irrevocably to a particular position on subsequent cases in violation of Canon 5(A)(3)(d)(ii).

Question 17.

D is the correct answer. The issue is client loyalty. The underlying principle is: a man may serve only one master. This principle is captured in Model Rule 1.9, dealing with conflicts between former and prospective clients. Model Rule 1.9(a) prohibits a lawyer from representing a prospective client in the same or a substantially related matter in which a former client has interests adverse to the interests of the prospective client without the former client's consent after consultation. On these facts, Attorney must refuse to represent Claimant because her claim is still pending and, obviously, she and Insurance Company have adverse interests. Option I is correct because it correctly states the controlling rule. Option IV is also correct. No rule prevents a lawyer from referring a client whom he cannot represent to another attorney who is not associated with the lawyer and who is competent. D correctly relies on I and IV.

A is incorrect. It depends on option I only, not both I and IV.

B is incorrect. It depends in part on option II, which is clearly wrong. Attorney may not represent Claimant on a pending claim against his former client.

C is incorrect. It depends in part on option III, which is wrong under the imputed disqualification principles of Model Rule 1.10. Model Rule 1.10(a) says: "While lawyers are associated in a firm, none of them shall knowingly represent a client when any one of them practicing alone would be prohibited from doing so by Rules 1.7 or 1.9."

Question 18.

D is the correct answer. Note that the facts have changed in two important respects. First, the original claim has been settled. Secondly, the present claim arises out of an entirely new set of facts which have no relationship to the original controversy. Model Rules 1.9 and 1.10 are not at issue unless the former and prospective clients have adverse interests "in the same or a substantially related matter" (Model Rule 1.9(a)), or unless the lawyer acquired information of the former client that is material to the present matter (Model Rule 1.9(b)(2)). On these facts, Attorney may exercise any of three options. He may refuse to discuss the matter. A lawyer is not compelled to undertake a representation if he does not wish to (option I). He may represent Claimant if he wishes because the "slip and fall" claim is new and unrelated to the former claim (option II). After rejecting the representation himself, he is free to refer Claimants to other lawyers who are not associated and are competent to handle the claim (option III).

A, B, and C are all incorrect because they reject one or another of the three permitted options available to Attorney.

Question 19.

D is the correct answer. The guiding rule is Model Rule 1.7, which deals with conflicts of interest. Unless Son is able to prove fraud and undue influence, we must assume that Client intended to cut Son's bequest in half. Thus, Son's position is directly adverse to Client's. If Client were still alive, Model Rule 1.7(a) would preclude representation of Son by attorney because the interests of two clients would be directly adverse to each other. Now that Client is dead, we are still constrained by Model Rule 1.7(a), which also directs a lawyer not to represent a client if representation of that client may be materially limited by the lawyer's responsibilities to another client or to a third person. (A deceased client is still a client for purpose of this Rule.) Note, also, that Attorney will necessarily be called as witness to execution of the will and the behavior and circumstances of the deceased Client. Because a lawyer may not act as advocate at a trial in which the lawyer is likely to be a necessary witness on a disputed issue (Model Rule 3.7), Attorney should not agree to represent Son in this will contest.

A is incorrect. Client's death does not trigger a release of Attorney from his duty of loyalty to Client. The second will is assumed to express Client's intent. The loyalty which Attorney owed to Client is transferred to Client's will, which Attorney prepared and witnessed.

B is incorrect. Although it correctly states one fact, that fact is immaterial to the issue raised by the entire fact pattern. The issue is the ability of a lawyer to represent two clients with directly adverse interests at the same time.

C is incorrect. First of all, it is incorrect on the law. A lawyer is not a guarantor of the validity of a will she prepares. Her job is to restate in legally sufficient form the intent of the testator and, if asked to do so, to supervise the proper execution of the will. Also, the statement is irrelevant to the issue raised by the facts.

Question 20.

C is the correct answer. The essence of our judicial system is the open and public development of facts and issues before jury and judge. This dictates against contact by either lawyer in a litigation with the judge or any juror which is not simultaneously or equally available to the other lawyer. The intent is to prevent undue influence by either side. Model Rule 3.5(a). Further, Model Rule 3.5(b) says specifically, "A lawyer shall not. . .communicate ex parte with such a person [judge, juror, prospective juror or other official] during the proceeding unless authorized to do so by law or court order." Here, however noble his intent, Attorney called Judge without advising his adversary that he would do. This was a direct violation of the rules.

A is incorrect. Ex parte contact with a judge is not permitted even if it ultimately leads to an argument by both sides. Obviously, an ex parte conversation between lawyer and the judge is not monitored for content. Although it may lead to open argument, it's always possible that some nuance or some ingredient in the original conversation has already worked its influence on the judge.

B is incorrect for the same basic reason as A. Ex parte contacts with judge or jury are prohibited, period.

D is incorrect. Whether or not the ex parte contact leads to a better result, it is prohibited. If it were not, we could never be certain that the record of a trial correctly reflected the testimony or the arguments which influenced the outcome.

Question 21.

A is the correct answer. It recognizes only one proper option for Alpha, option I. Under this option, Attorney recognizes that he is not permitted any communication with Plaintiff because Plaintiff is represented by Beta. Model Rule 4.2 says: "In representing a client, a lawyer shall not communicate about the subject of the representation with a person the lawyer knows to be represented by another lawyer in the matter, unless the lawyer has the consent of the other lawyer or is authorized to do so by law or a court order." This is known as the "no-contact" rule. Obviously, here, Plaintiff is represented by Beta who has not been consulted about the contact between Alpha and Plaintiff.

B is incorrect. It adopts option II. Although option II may appear to be an innocent response by Alpha to Plaintiff's suggestion, it does represent improper communication. Beta has been involved in all the settlement discussions. It's improper to suggest to Beta's client that Beta be ignored in a direct negotiation between the two litigants. It's not improper for the parties to a matter to speak to each other voluntarily without consulting their lawyers, but it is improper for a lawyer for one side to suggest to the other party that he bypass his lawyer, even in a settlement discussion. On the other hand, there's nothing to prevent a lawyer from suggesting to his own client that settlement discussions may be enhanced by direct contact between the client and the adverse party. See ABA Formal Opinion 92-362 (1992).

C is incorrect. It depends on II and III, which are both wrong. We've seen why II is wrong and III is wrong because it constitutes communication between Alpha and Plaintiff, a represented party.

D is incorrect. It relies in part on II and III.

Question 22.

C is the correct answer. It is clear that a lawyer may advertise her services. This right was confirmed by the Supreme Court in *Bates v. State Bar of Arizona*, 433 U.S. 350 (1977). The right is incorporated in Model Rule 7.2, which enables a lawyer to advertise by any public medium or through written or recorded communication. The right is subject, however, to Model Rules 7.1 and 7.3. Model Rule 7.1 imposes the requirement that the advertisement not be false or misleading. Generally, so long as the statements in the advertisement are truthful, the ad passes muster. Model Rule 7.3 forbids direct solicitation either in-person or by telephone. Here, no part of the law firm's ad would seem to be anything more than a statement of simple facts about the firm.

A is not correct. The advertisement need not state the lawyer's qualifications. On the contrary, a lawyer who ventures to state her qualifications risks the possibility that she will overblow them. Comment [2] to Model Rule 7.2 lists some of the matters a lawyer may list with impunity: name, address, telephone number, range of services, basis for fees, foreign language ability, references and, with their consent, names of clients.

B is not correct. Nothing in this ad can reasonably be construed as encouraging litigation.

D is not correct. Many radio and television stations can be heard in states adjoining the place of FCC license. As long as a lawyer licensed in one state does not state that he is able to practice in a state in which he is not licensed, it will be assumed that his ad is directed only at listeners and viewers in the state in which he is licensed.

Question 23.

C is the correct answer. Under Model Rule 7.2, lawyers are permitted to advertise, subject to Model Rule 7.1, which prohibits a lawyer from making false or misleading statements about her services, and Model Rule 7.3, which limits direct contact with prospective clients. So long as there are no false or misleading statements in Attorney's advertisement, he would not be subject to discipline for placing this ad.

A is incorrect. It refers to Model Rule 7.3(a), which prohibits a lawyer from making *an in person or live telephone or real-time electronic contact* with a prospective client unless the lawyer has had a prior relationship with the prospective client. This situation deals with written advertising, so answer A is a red herring.

B is incorrect. There is no reason Attorney shouldn't use a coupon in his advertisement.

D is incorrect. The issue here is whether the advertisement meets the requirements of the rules. Attorney is placing a general written advertisement and has no way of knowing whether a person is currently represented by a lawyer.

Question 24.

D is the correct answer. Ordinarily, a lawyer is duty-bound to report another lawyer's violation of the Model Rules of Professional Conduct if the violation raises a substantial question as to that lawyer's honesty, trustworthiness or fitness as a lawyer. Model Rule 8.3. However, when the information about the violation is protected under the client confidentiality rules of Model Rule 1.6, this duty is no longer absolute but discretionary. But Comment [2] to Model Rule 8.3 advises: "However, a lawyer should encourage a client to consent to disclosure where prosecution would not substantially prejudice the client's interests." On these facts, which show that Client would be reluctant to report Beta because he is an old friend, Alpha would probably be wasting his breath to encourage the disclosure of Beta's neglect of Client's interests to the disciplinary authorities. Alpha will not be subject to discipline if he chooses not to report Beta without Client's consent.

A is incorrect. Whether or not Alpha believes Beta was guilty of professional misconduct for failing to perform the services for which he was retained, he will not be subject to discipline if he chooses not to report Beta without Client's consent.

B is incorrect. In the absence of the Model Rule 1.6 confidentiality issue, Alpha's belief as to Beta's usual conduct would be immaterial. The duty to report another lawyer's misconduct of which a lawyer has knowledge is absolute, not discretionary. Once an act of misconduct is known, it becomes a matter for the "appropriate professional authority," not for any lawyer. Only the fact that Client has not consented to the disclosure gives Alpha the option whether or not to report Beta.

C is incorrect. The trigger which converts Alpha's duty from an absolute duty to a discretionary option is the lack of Client consent, not the level of Client's satisfaction with Beta or the fact that Client was not out of money.

Question 25.

C is the correct answer. All of the choices except option I apply to the situation. Partners in a law firm (not the firm itself) must make reasonable efforts to make sure all lawyers in the firm comply with the Rules of Professional Conduct, Model Rule 5.1(a) and are subject to discipline if they do not. The partners of Alpha & Beta have not made any efforts at all to institute a system to ensure compliance with the Rules as required under Model Rule 5.1 and would therefore be subject to discipline. Associate would be subject to discipline under Model Rule 8.4 for misconduct involving "dishonesty, fraud, deceit, or misrepresentation." Both the law firm and Associate would be subject to a negligence-based malpractice claim, because Client did not receive competent representation (Model Rule 1.1) due to associate's inexperience and lack of supervision.

A is incorrect because it does not incorporate III.

B is incorrect because it relies in part on I, which is incorrect, and does not rely on II.

D is incorrect because it relies in part on I, which is incorrect.

Question 26.

C is the correct answer. The answer recognizes that options I and III are both proper but that option II is not. No rule is more sacred or more frequently the root of lawyer misconduct than Model Rule 1.15, which covers a lawyer's duty to safekeep the money and property of a client or of third persons that are in the possession of the lawyer. The Rule has two essential components: (1) Client money and property must be held separately from the lawyer's own—i.e., commingling is forbidden. Client funds must be kept in a separate account and client property must be identified as such "and appropriately safeguarded." (2) When a lawyer receives funds or property belonging to the client, the lawyer must notify the client and "promptly deliver to the client. . .any funds or other property that the client. . .is entitled to receive." Here, Attorney has received a settlement check the proceeds of which belong to Plaintiff. (We are not told that Attorney has any interest in the proceeds, as for fees or disbursements.) It is proper for him to endorse the check because this constitutes negotiation or payment to Plaintiff. (It may be more prudent, however, to deposit the check in the Client Trust Account to make sure that it clears.) It is also proper to deposit the check in a Client Trust Account, advise the client and then forward the entire proceeds to Plaintiff.

A is incorrect. Although it recognizes option I as proper, it rejects option III which is also proper.

B is incorrect. It recognizes option III, but not option I.

D is incorrect. Although it recognizes options I and III, both of which are correct, it is the only answer which adopts option II, which is clearly wrong and would subject Attorney to severe discipline. Deposit of the check into Attorney's personal account would constitute commingling with Attorney's own funds. The violation is not cured even by the immediate mailing of Attorney's check to Plaintiff. Model Rule 1.15, Comment [1].

Question 27.

D is the correct answer. In construing the propriety of a lawyer's contribution in a judicial election campaign, the ABA Model Rules and the ABA Code of Judicial Conduct must be read in tandem. Model Rule 3.5 prohibits a lawyer from seeking to influence a judge or juror. Comment [1] to Model Rule 3.5 says: "Many forms of improper influence upon a tribunal [. . .] are specified in the ABA Model Code of Judicial Conduct, with which an advocate should be familiar." The cases and the disciplinary rulings in all states almost invariably construe a loan or gift to a judge by a lawyer who appears before him as an attempt to influence the judge. Thus, a contribution to Beta's campaign may not be made by a gift to Beta personally under Model Rule 3.5. Further, Canon 5(C)(2) of the Code of Judicial Conduct begins, "A candidate shall not personally solicit or accept campaign contributions or personally solicit publicly stated support." The provision goes on to permit the establishment of "a committee of responsible persons" to conduct the candidate's campaign and allows the committee to solicit and accept reasonable campaign contributions and public support from lawyers. D correctly recognizes that Alpha may make his contribution to Beta's campaign committee.

A is incorrect. Alpha may not give the contribution to Alpha personally. The underlying reason for the rule prohibiting personal gifts directly to the candidate is that it will lead to excessive influence by the donor lawyer when he appears before the judge.

B is incorrect. The rules do not require that the gift be made anonymously, only that it not be made to the judge personally. A donation to the judge's duly constituted campaign committee is perfectly proper.

C is incorrect. A lawyer may contribute to a judge's campaign committee whether or not he appears before the judge. If you think about it, you will recognize that lawyers who appear before a judge are better able than others to determine whether the judge is really qualified.

Question 28.

D is the correct answer. Under Model Rule 4.1, a lawyer shall not knowingly make a false statement of material fact to a third party. However, under generally accepted negotiating conventions, certain kinds of statements, including estimates of profits and values, are not taken as statements of material fact. Model Rule 4.1, Comment [2].

Attorney's statement about the profits of the ice cream parlor during negotiations would not subject him to discipline.

A is incorrect. Attorney has not made a false statement of material fact as defined in the Rules.

B is incorrect. Again, in the course of negotiating, a certain amount of exaggeration is to be expected and is acceptable.

C is incorrect. This choice hints at the lawyer's duty to "act with commitment and dedication to the interests of the client." Model Rule 1.3, Comment [1]. The issue here, however, is whether Attorney made a false statement of material fact and therefore should be subject to discipline. If he did make such a statement, it would be improper and he would be subject to discipline regardless of whether he had done so for the benefit of his client.

Question 29.

B is the correct answer. The question requires an analysis of the standards which determine whether a lawyer has been diligent and prompt in representing the client. The standards are set by Model Rule 1.3 which says: "An attorney shall act with reasonable diligence and promptness in representing a client." Comment [2] says, "...A lawyer's work load must be controlled so that each matter can be handled competently." Comment [3] says: "Perhaps no professional shortcoming is more widely resented than procrastination...[]when a lawyer overlooks a statute of limitations, the client's legal position may be destroyed. Even when a client's interests are not affected in substance, however, unreasonable delay can cause a client needless anxiety and undermine confidence in the lawyer's trustworthiness." The facts here show the typical course ending in a lawyer's discipline: (1) make appointments and ignore them; (2) ignore a client's phone calls and requests for information and progress reports; (3) fail to keep the client advised; (4) work on other matters to the exclusion or neglect of client; (5) ignore the passage of time and the inevitable running of the statute of limitations. The key word in Answer

B is "neglect." Alpha has been guilty of professional neglect. After misuse of client funds, this is the most common basis for lawyer discipline.

A is incorrect. Commitment to one or several clients to the neglect of another is exactly what Model Rule 1.3 was intended to prevent.

C is incorrect. Alpha is not relieved of the consequences of her neglect because Passenger avoids the running of the statute. Passenger has already suffered in other ways. First of all, if Alpha had pursued her settlement negotiations, Passenger might have enjoyed the proceeds of settlement many months earlier. Secondly, the attitude of the bus company may have hardened in the interim and made settlement more difficult. Also, Passenger would have been spared the anguish and frustration caused by unanswered phone calls and worry about her claim.

D is incorrect. The issue is not the retainer but Alpha's neglect of Passenger's interests. If Alpha had not returned the money, however, she would have faced another basis for discipline.

Question 30.

C is the correct answer. The question raises issues under the Rules controlling lawyer advocacy of a client's interests. Model Rule 3.2 directs a lawyer to make reasonable efforts to expedite litigation consistent with the interests of the client. Model Rule 1.3 directs a lawyer to act with reasonable diligence and promptness in representing a client. If Alpha had not known that Beta represented Insco, there would be no issue here at all. Does Alpha's knowledge that Beta is involved require him to call Beta before entering a default judgment? The answer is no. Nothing in the Rules requires Alpha to call Beta. Model Rule 3.4 does require that an attorney be fair to opposing counsel. The list of items constituting unfair conduct does not include the requirement to advise opposing counsel before entering an order or judgment on default. Such a requirement would impose restraints on a lawyer's action which might ultimately injure the client.

A is incorrect. As we have explained above, Alpha's knowledge that Beta was Insco's attorney did not create an obligation by Alpha to inform Beta of the default judgment.

B is incorrect. If Alpha knew Beta and had dealt with him in other matters, it might have been preferable to advise Beta before entering the default in order to avoid Beta's wrath and a motion to reopen, but nothing required Alpha to do so.

D is incorrect. First of all, it is not responsive to the question. Secondly, each step in a litigation requires prompt action by a lawyer. Whether or not Insco is good for the money, Alpha must protect his client's interests at every step.

Question 31.

C is the correct answer. Candidates for judicial office must observe the provisions of the Code of Judicial Conduct governing judicial campaigns and elections. Most of these provisions are contained in Canon 5(A)(3). Canon 5(A)(3)(d)(iii) provides: "A candidate for a judicial office:. . .shall not. . .knowingly misrepresent the identity, qualifications, present position or other fact concerning the candidate or an opponent. . ." The word "knowingly" is one of the terms defined in the Terminology preceding the Code. The definition is: " 'Knowingly,' 'knowledge,' 'known' or 'knows' denotes actual knowledge of the fact in question. A person's knowledge may be inferred from circumstances. . ." Here, Attorney does not have actual knowledge that Judge was not reprimanded for misconduct in office. Nor was it unreasonable for her to rely on the statement of an official directly responsible for maintaining the information at issue.

A is incorrect. It assumes that Attorney had a duty to inquire into the records themselves after getting a response to her inquiry from the director of the commission himself. This was not a reasonable requirement to impose upon attorney.

B is incorrect. The test is not the truth of the statement but whether Attorney has knowledge of the truth.

D is incorrect. The answer suggests that judges are held to a different standard in contested elections than in non-contested elections. But even in a contested judicial election, there are constraints upon the candidates that do not apply to candidates for non-judicial offices. See Canon 5.

Question 32.

B is the correct answer. Lawyers are officers of the court and are charged with the responsibility not to make statements with reckless disregard for the truth concerning the qualifications or integrity of a judge. Model Rule 8.2. Comment [1] points out that false statements by a lawyer can undermine public confidence in the administration of justice. Here, Attorney has impugned the integrity not only of one judge but of the entire judiciary. Especially because his work as a skilled litigator brings him before these very judges, who decide both fact and law, the inescapable inference is that he has special influence over them.

A is incorrect. A lawyer may contribute to a judge's campaign committee without accounting for his motivation in doing so. The Code of Judicial Conduct permits the campaign committees of judges to solicit funds from lawyers. But the funds may not be used for the private benefit of the candidates.

C is incorrect. If the statements are indeed true, then Attorney is subject to discipline under Model Rule 3.5 for seeking "to influence a judge, juror, prospective juror or other official by means prohibited by law."

D is incorrect. It's immaterial to Attorney's misconduct that the prospective client did not retain him.

Question 33.

D is the correct answer. At the heart of our legal system is the confidence by each side in a controversy that no fact and no issue of law will be considered by the trier except on an open record which is available to both sides. Each side is entitled to know and to respond to every fact and every argument presented by the other side. If a judge could consult any legal source he wished without identifying it and giving each side the right to respond, our adversarial system would be reduced to chaos. At the same time, there are instances in which a judge will need to get advice on the law, especially when, as in these facts, the lawyers have not cleared up all the issues. To enable the judge to do this without subverting the adversarial process, Canon 3(B)(7)(b) permits a judge to "obtain the advice of a disinterested expert on the law applicable to a proceeding before the judge if the judge gives notice to the parties of the person consulted and the substance of the advice, and affords the parties reasonable opportunity to respond."

A is incorrect. It's not enough that the expert consulted by the judge be impartial. The parties are entitled to know what the expert has been asked and what he's advised. After all, the expert may be wrong or the judge may not have communicated the issues correctly. The parties may want to respond, and they must be given the opportunity to do so.

B is incorrect. It begs the issue. We have to assume that a judge will not ask for advice if he doesn't think it's needed in the interest of justice. What's at issue here is not the judge's integrity but the very process by which adversarial issues are determined in our judicial process.

C is wrong only because it doesn't correspond with the way in which the framers of the Code of Judicial Conduct decided to resolve this issue. They might have insisted on the prior consent of the parties, but they chose instead to make it possible for the judge to reach for advice so long as he tells the parties what he's doing and gives them the opportunity to respond.

Question 34.

D is the correct answer. The key to this question is the statement, "all of which is true." The controlling Rules are Model Rules 7.1 and 7.2. Model Rule 7.2 permits a lawyer to advertise her services to the public, subject to Model Rules 7.1 and 7.3. Model Rule 7.3 deals with in-person solicitation and solicitation by phone, mail and recordings and is not relevant to these facts, which deal with newspaper advertising. Model Rule 7.1, which is relevant, requires only that the content of an ad not be false or misleading. The underlying support for lawyer advertising is a string of Supreme Court cases resisting controls over commercial speech, including advertising. The only limit on a lawyer's ads is that they must not contain a material misrepresentation of fact or law.

A is incorrect. It cites choice III, which is a perfectly proper reference to the lawyer's ability to deal efficiently with Greek-speaking clients. So long as the statement is true, it is not objectionable.

B is incorrect. Neither Statement I nor Statement II is a basis for discipline. Both are truthful statements of Attorney's educational qualifications and his office hours, all facts which the client would want to know.

C is incorrect because it refers to all three statements as bases for discipline, and, as we have seen, they are all perfectly proper because they are true and they do not fall outside the limits permitted under Model Rule 7.1.

Question 35.

B is the correct answer. Because Attorney is newly admitted, he may not realize that he's become party to a scheme that enables Trustco to engage in the unauthorized practice of law.

Model Rule 5.5(a) says quite simply, "A lawyer shall not practice law in a jurisdiction in violation of the regulation of the legal profession in that jurisdiction or assist another in doing so." Without Attorney's participation, Trustco would not be able to present its customers with completed documents ready for signature. Attorney is enabling Trustco's officer to discuss and "work out" the details of trusts and wills, functions which clearly fall within the parameters of law practice. Attorney is also aiding Trustco and its officer to misrepresent to the customer the way in which the documents are being prepared. The arrangement between Attorney and Trustco is in the nature of a partnership, and Model Rule 5.4(b) prevents a lawyer from forming a partnership with a non-lawyer if the function of the partnership is the practice of law. Also, even if Attorney is not sharing in the bank's fees directly, he is in effect doing so by getting free office space. Model Rule 5.4(a) prohibits fee-splitting with non-lawyers. Attorney is subject to discipline.

A is incorrect. Don't be confused by the phrase "restricting the right to practice." It may suggest to you the restrictions against a lawyer's right to practice which are contained in Model Rule 5.6. But Model Rule 5.6 deals with restrictions imposed by restrictive employment agreements between a lawyer and his partners or law firm and by settlement agreements resolving controversies between private parties. Except for these provisions, which are intended to prevent economic pressure on a lawyer either to gain or keep employment or to settle a pending matter, there are no rules preventing a lawyer from restricting the range or extent of his practice.

C is incorrect. A lawyer is not required to charge a client for his services. The problem here is not the failure to charge but the barrier which has been placed by Trustco between its customers and Attorney. Attorney is permitting himself to practice, in effect, through agents who are not and cannot be under his direct supervision.

D is incorrect. Attorney is, in effect, giving advice to Trustco's customers. Or, at least, he is participating in an arrangement which enables persons who are not authorized to practice law to give legal advice.

Question 36.

C is the correct answer. A lawyer who represents both husband and wife in any matter in which the husband and wife have a mutual interest is always treading on thin ice, especially in these days of relative impermanence in marital relationships. Here, Attorney has represented both Husband and Wife in a business transaction and then in resolving a business dispute between them. Each is a former client. As such, each is entitled to the protective umbrella of Model Rule 1.9. Model Rule 1.9(a) says that a lawyer who has formerly represented a client in a matter shall not thereafter represent another person in the same or a substantially related matter in which that person's interests are materially adverse to the interests of the former client unless the former client consents after consultation. Further, a lawyer who has formerly represented a client in a matter may not use information relating to the former representation to the disadvantage of the former client (with exceptions not relevant here). Model Rule 1.9(c)(1). Under these facts, Attorney may not represent Wife in litigation against the Husband.

A is incorrect. This answer may lead you to think (mistakenly) that a former client loses his right to prevent a lawyer who represents a co-client from representing the co-client in an action adverse to him simply because he and his co-client have shared their confidences with each other and with the lawyer. This is not the case. Model Rule 1.9 still applies to these facts.

B is incorrect. The Rule against representing a current client in an action adverse to the interests of a former client protects all former clients, whatever the facts.

D is incorrect. Again, Model Rule 1.9 was designed to protect a former client against an adverse action on behalf of a current or prospective client. That the former client is now represented by new counsel is irrelevant to the application of the Rule.

Question 37.

D is the correct answer. Alpha may properly engage in all these activities. Note that the facts test the activities of lawyer Alpha, not judicial candidate Beta. A lawyer may support the candidacy of one judicial candidate over another so long as he does not seek to influence the judge "by means prohibited by law." Model Rule 3.5(a). Generally, a lawyer may contribute to a judge's campaign and solicit contributions from other attorneys. But he must do so in a way that cannot be reasonably interpreted as an effort to influence the candidate as judge. A lawyer who wishes to help a judicial candidate must also consult the Code of Judicial Conduct, which describes conduct that suggests improper influence. For example, CJC Canon 5(C)(2) prevents a judicial candidate from soliciting or accepting campaign contributions personally. Instead, the contributions must be solicited and collected only by a "committee of responsible persons" supporting the judge. A lawyer who contributed personally to a candidate for an elected judicial office would be helping the candidate to violate this Rule and would be subject to discipline. Alpha may engage in the activities described in II because the contribution are being made to Beta's campaign committee. Alpha also has the right to engage in the activities described in I and III. These are activities that come under the constitutional umbrella of freedom of thought and freedom of expression. Lawyers are uniquely qualified to judge the qualifications of candidates for judicial office. Their participation in the democratic process by which judges are elected should be encouraged.

A, B, and C are all incorrect because each excludes either one or two of the correct options.

Question 38.

A is the correct answer. A lawyer may advertise her services in the same media as any other professional or merchant. The right has been confirmed by the Supreme Court (*Bates v. State Bar of Arizona*, 433 U.S. 350 (1977)), and is codified in Model Rule 7.2. There are, however, special limitations that apply only to lawyers. The most important is embodied in Model Rule 7.1. The Rule requires that the lawyer not make a misleading statement about herself or her services. A statement is misleading if it contains a material misrepresentation of fact or law; omits a fact which will make the statement not misleading; is likely to create unjustified expectations about the results the lawyer is likely to achieve; or compares the lawyer's services with other lawyers' services without substantiation in fact. The ad televised by attorney here meets all of these requirements on its face. Even the last sentence is not objectionable. It suggests only that Attorney may have a relatively low fee schedule or that potential clients may have a mistaken notion about the level of legal fees in Attorney's area. Also, Attorney is complying with the requirement to maintain copies of all her ads.

B is incorrect. The ad does not state that Attorney's fees are lower than those generally charged in her area, only that the potential client may have a mistaken notion about legal fees in general. Further, a statement that Attorney's fees were lower than those generally charged in her area would not be improper if the statement could be supported by the facts.

C is incorrect. Nothing in the Rules prevents a lawyer from using professional actors to read a radio or TV ad. The actor is obviously not pretending to be the Attorney; he is simply conveying her message in the same way as in other TV ads. If a lawyer did instruct an actor to pretend to be the lawyer when reading the ad, that, of course, would represent a material misrepresentation of fact and would be disciplinable.

D is incorrect. Nothing in the Rules prohibits a lawyer from charging for an initial consultation and nothing in the ad suggests that Attorney will not charge for the consultation.

Question 39.

D is the correct answer. Prosecutors are expected to observe all the Rules governing lawyers, and then some. One of the Rules is addressed only to prosecutors. See Model Rule 3.8. One Rule that has raised debate by prosecutors is the no-contact rule — Model Rule 4.2. This Rule prohibits contact by a lawyer about the subject matter of a representation with a client known to have another lawyer, without the consent of that other lawyer or unless authorized by law. Many prosecutors, especially federal prosecutors, have argued that this Rule should not prevent them for contacting another lawyer's client to facilitate an investigation into criminal conduct. But the ABA and most courts have not agreed, and the no-contact rule in Model Rule 4.2 is still effective against prosecutors. Option I is therefore unacceptable. Prosecutor may not send a member of his staff to consult with Deft without Attorney's knowledge and consent. But prosecutor is free to adopt both option II and option III. Because he believes that justice will be served by amending the indictment to the offense of joy riding, he may exercise his discretion to offer the new charge. On the other hand, he is not compelled to withdraw the original indictment and may proceed to trial on the charge of auto theft. If he does proceed to trial, he is obligated to proceed vigorously.

A, B, and C are all incorrect because each either includes option I, which is wrong, or excludes either option II or option III, both of which are right.

Question 40.

C is the correct answer. Although Model Rule 8.3 makes the obligation to report another lawyer's professional misconduct mandatory, the definition of the term "professional misconduct" as applied to a particular case can be elusive. Model Rule 8.3 defines professional misconduct as "a violation of the Rules of Professional Conduct that raises a substantial question as to that lawyer's honesty, trustworthiness or fitness as a lawyer." But Comment [3] to Model Rule 8.3 says, "This Rule limits the reporting obligation to those offenses that a self-regulating profession must vigorously endeavor to prevent. A measure of judgment is, therefore, required in complying with the provisions of this Rule." These facts tell us only that Prosecutor suspects that Attorney is acting in his own interests instead of Deft's interests. A mere suspicion is not enough to warrant a disciplinary complaint. Prosecutor should not refer his suspicions of Attorney's motives until they are confirmed by specific proof. When and if the proof surfaces, Prosecutor will have an affirmative obligation to report Attorney's conduct. Under Model Rule 1.7(a), an attorney may not represent a client if the representation may be materially limited by the lawyer's own interests unless the lawyer reasonably believes the client will not be adversely affected or unless the client consents after consultation. If the Prosecutor had proof that Attorney's real motive was to advance her own candidacy to the detriment of the client's interests, he would be required to report her to the disciplinary authorities.

A is incorrect. The test for one lawyer's obligation to report another is not his estimate of the quality of the other lawyer's work or the impact on that lawyer's client. Considering the tension than can arise between lawyers in an adversarial system, it would be imprudent to give a lawyer the power to report his adversary for anything but true professional misconduct.

B is incorrect. Again, the fact that widespread publicity accompanies a high-profile case does not go to proof of a lawyer's motives. Especially when intent is at issue, the proof of misconduct must be clear and persuasive. The impact upon a lawyer of a charge of professional misconduct is serious and lasting, and the Rules are intended to protect lawyers against indiscriminate allegations.

D is incorrect. Whether or not Attorney was zealous or competent, a conflict between his own interests and Deft's interests would be grounds for complaint. Model Rule 1.7 imposes its requirements at the start of a representation. It begins, "A lawyer shall not represent a client. . ."

Question 41.

A is the correct answer. The question illustrates the tension between Attorney's duty not to reveal information obtained from the client unless the client consents after consultation (Model Rule 1.6) and Attorney's duty not to use or offer false evidence (Model Rule 3.3(a)(3). The choice is between the duty of confidentiality and the duty to maintain candor toward the court. In general, the conflict should be resolved in favor of candor to the tribunal. Although the rule of confidentiality "contributes to the trust that is the hallmark of the lawyer-client relationship [and encourages the client] to seek legal assistance and to communicate fully and frankly with the lawyer" (Model Rule 1.6, Comment [2]), the rule is subject to limited exceptions.

First, the lawyer may not counsel or assist a client in conduct that is criminal or fraudulent. See Model Rule 1.2(d). Similarly, a lawyer has a duty under Model Rule 3.3(a)(3) not to use false evidence. This duty is essentially a special instance of the duty prescribed in Model Rule 1.2(d) to avoid assisting a client in criminal or fraudulent conduct. When Attorney in this Question asked the client for his name, he knew that the response would be a falsehood which would mislead the court in its judgment of Driver's offense. Attorney is subject to discipline under Model Rule 3.3(a)(3).

B is incorrect. It's immaterial to Attorney's duty to the court whether Driver committed a felony or a lesser crime. The point is the testimony would mislead the court into administering a lighter sentence than the law required.

C is incorrect. It begs the issue. We know that the information would ordinarily be protected because it was disclosed to Attorney as a confidence during the course of representation. But it cannot be protected if the consequence is the presentation of testimony which is known to Attorney to be false. The duty of candor to the tribunal trumps the duty of confidentiality to Driver.

D is incorrect. The name is an issue in the trial. If Driver's true name is used, he's subject to the heavier penalty. If the court doesn't learn his true name, Driver gets the lighter penalty. In one case, the court is misled; in the other, it isn't.

Question 42.

A is the correct answer. The ultimate goal of our adversarial judicial system is to enable the trier of fact to receive truthful testimony. Long before the Model Rules were drafted, the common law of most states provided that it was improper to pay a witness any fee in consideration of his testimony. The ABA Model Code which antedated the ABA Model Rules was very explicit in enjoining a lawyer from paying any compensation to a witness contingent on the outcome of the trial. However, under the Code, a lawyer was permitted to pay the expenses incurred by the witness in attending and testifying, as well as reasonable compensation to the witness for his loss of time. This problem is treated in Model Rule 3.4, which provides, "A lawyer shall not:...(b) offer an inducement to a witness that is prohibited by law." Comment [3] to the Rule tells us, "With regard to Paragraph (b), it is not improper to pay a witness's expenses..." Model Rule 3.4(b) has been interpreted to permit only reimbursement for actual expenses while attending the trial, including travel expenses and reasonable compensation for the witness' loss of time — i.e., wages. Choices I and II correctly restate this interpretation of the Rule. They are the only choices which are correct (see below). Because option A eliminates only Choice III, it is the correct answer.

B is incorrect because it depends on in part on Choice III, which is wrong for the reasons stated.

C is incorrect because it also depends in part on Choice III.

D is incorrect because it concludes that Attorney is not subject to discipline under any of the options. As we have seen, he is subject to discipline under III.

Question 43.

A is the correct answer. A judge's extra-judicial activities are always subject to scrutiny in order to "minimize the risk of conflict with judicial obligations." Model Code of Judicial Conduct, Canon 4. On the other hand, it would be unrealistic to expect judges to live as hermits in isolation. Canon 4(C)(3) permits a judge to serve as an officer, director, trustee, or non-legal advisor of an "educational, religious, charitable, fraternal or civic organization not conducted for profit..." (Note that the judge is precluded from giving any legal advice to the organization.) But the judge may not serve an organization that is engaged in a proceeding that is likely to come before the judge or that is engaged frequently in adversary proceedings in the court of which the judge is a member. Canon 4(C)(3)(a). Canon 4(D)(5)(a) permits a judge to accept "a gift incident to a public testimonial," as well as "books, tapes and other resource materials supplied by publishers on a complimentary basis for official use..." However, there are limitations on testimonials. The Commentary to Canon 4(D)(5)(a) says that a judge may accept a testimonial from an organization only if that organization is not an organization whose members comprise or frequently represent the same side in litigation. Also, the organization must not be one which is likely to come before the judge. On these facts, Judge may accept the portrait.

B is incorrect. The fact that judge did not receive compensation is only one piece of the puzzle. Other pieces are also required to make the gift proper: (a) that it is a public testimonial; (b) by a charitable organization; (c) which does not engage in litigation before the judge's court. (Note: a judge may receive compensation for activities permitted under Canon 4 if the source of payment does not give the appearance of influencing the judge in his judicial duties and if the compensation is reasonable and does not exceed what a non-judge would receive for the same activity. Canon 4(H)).

C is incorrect. There is no specific limit in the Code for the cost of a testimonial gift. The test is whether the value of the gift is so excessive as to suggest undue influence either in a specific matter or generally, and, also, whether the source of the gift is suspect. (On this issue, see the next paragraph.)

D is incorrect. A testimonial gift from lawyers to a judge is not prohibited per se. However, there are some restrictions. The lawyers may not comprise an organization which frequently represents the same side in litigation — e.g., an association of personal injury lawyers. Commentary, Canon 4(D)(5)(a). Also, if the lawyers have come or are likely to come before the judge and the value of the gift exceeds $150, the judge must report the gift.

Question 44.

C is the correct answer. A lawyer in litigation is expected to be a zealous advocate of his client's position. If he is called to testify on a contested issue of fact, his role as advocate becomes confused. Also, his testimony may create an irreconcilable conflict of interest between the client and himself. For these reasons, a lawyer is prohibited from acting as advocate in a matter if he is likely to be called as a witness.

There are three exceptions: (1) the testimony relates to an uncontested issue; (2) the testimony relates to the nature and value of the lawyer's services in the matter; and (3) the lawyer's disqualification would work substantial hardship on the client. Model Rule 3.7. The potential for damage is so great that the rule may not be waived by the client. Because the facts here do not present an exception to the general rule, Attorney may not represent the Executor. Executor may retain other counsel and Attorney will then be free to testify about the Testator's competence. These facts, by the way, show why a lawyer should never act as subscribing witness to a will he himself prepares. When a lawyer prepares a will and then acts as subscribing witness, he knows that he may later be called to appear as witness in a contest of the will.

A is incorrect. It restates the problem, not the solution. It's exactly because he is likely to be called as a witness that he may not represent Executor. True, there is some hardship on the Executor in forcing him to find and retain other counsel in order to prove the will, but the problem is not insurmountable. On balance, the need to forestall participation by the lawyer as both advocate and witness is paramount.

B is incorrect. The rule against the lawyer as witness assumes that the lawyer would testify in support of his client. "The problem can arise whether the lawyer is called as a witness on behalf of his client or is called by the opposing party." Model Rule 3.7, Comment [6].

D is incorrect. It states correctly the underlying rationale for the rule, but not the rule itself. Whether or not Attorney's testimony supports one side or another, he may not represent either side if he is likely to be called as a necessary witness.

Question 45.

A is the correct answer. In settling a claim or potential claim for malpractice, a lawyer must advise an unrepresented client in writing of the desirability of seeking independent legal counsel. Model Rule 1.8(h)(2).

B is incorrect. Attorney's belief, or even whether the agreement is fair or unfair to the Buyer, is not the issue. In this situation, under the Rules, the lawyer must advise the client in writing of the appropriateness of independent representation and must give the client ample time to find and consult with another lawyer.

C is incorrect. There is no prohibition on settling a potential malpractice claim, whether or not a related matter is ongoing.

D is incorrect. The Rules do not require that Buyer actually be separately represented, only that he be advised in writing of the desirability of seeking independent legal counsel and given time to consult with another lawyer.

Question 46.

D is the correct answer. None of the actions in I, II, or III would subject Alpha to discipline. Under Model Rule 7.2, lawyers are permitted to advertise, subject to Model Rule 7.1, which prohibits a lawyer from making false or misleading statements about her services, and Model Rule 7.3, which limits direct contact with prospective clients. The statements in Alpha's flyer are accurate and meet the requirement of Model Rule 7.2 that the advertisement contain her office address. In order to assist the public in obtaining legal services, a lawyer "may advertise services through written, recorded or electronic communication..." Model Rule 7.2(a) and Comment [1]. The rule permits dissemination of the lawyer's name, address, and telephone number; the sorts of services she will undertake, information about fees, and credit and payment arrangements, among other things Model Rule 7.2, Comment [2]. All of Alpha's actions certainly fall within the parameters set by Model Rule 7.2, therefore option D is the correct answer because it relies on I, II, and III all being acceptable under the Rules.

A is incorrect because III would not be prohibited. Alpha has simply placed a temporary sign on her van that identifies it as the van described in the advertisement.

B is incorrect because neither I nor II would subject Alpha to discipline. Alpha's flyers meet the requirements of the Rules and placing them in the booths of the artists would certainly be a permitted form of dissemination. Placing a retainer agreement on the back of the flyer is a way of conveying payment terms, which is allowed under the Rules.

C is incorrect because neither I, II, or III would subject Alpha to discipline.

Question 47.

D is the correct answer. In making decisions and exercising options, a lawyer is required to act with competence. Model Rule 1.1. This means that he must employ "the legal knowledge, skill, thoroughness and preparation reasonably necessary for the representation." In other words, he is not a guarantor of a successful outcome or even of a consequence-free result. He is required, however, to exercise his judgment in a manner that would be considered reasonable by other lawyers under all the circumstances. There are circumstances in which a lawyer may reasonably advise a client not to respond to questions by a legislative fact-finding committee, even when the client is faced by the risk of imprisonment. These facts do not tell us what the underlying facts were, but they do state clearly that Attorney "reasonably believed" that it was in the best interests of Witness not to answer. Attorney is not subject to discipline so long as he acted reasonably.

A is incorrect. Whether or not Attorney ultimately made the right decision, he cannot be disciplined because he acted upon a reasonable belief that he was protecting Witness. There is no suggestion in the facts that Attorney was not competent to represent Witness before the committee or to exercise his reasonable discretion to advise Witness not to answer.

B is incorrect. The facts do not disclose the constitutional basis for the refusal by Witness to answer the committee's questions. Obviously, however, the consequences to the Witness in failing to exercise her constitutional rights were deemed by Attorney to be more serious and severe than the refusal to answer. Although the general rule is that an attorney may not counsel a client to engage, or assist a client, in conduct that the lawyer knows is criminal (Model Rule 1.2), most courts would support Witness' right to refuse to answer if her constitutional rights were in jeopardy.

C is incorrect. Model Rule 1.2 does not distinguish between crimes involving moral turpitude and other crimes. A lawyer is not supposed to assist a client in any crime, however characterized. However, the conflict between the need to protect a constitutional right not to answer and the obligation to observe a law requiring an answer is irreconcilable. The lawyer's obligation under these circumstances is to advise the client of the consequences of each alternative.

Question 48.

D is the correct answer. A lawyer must always keep the property of clients separate from the lawyer's own property. Model Rule 1.15. Funds should be deposited in a separate client trust account. It would therefore be improper for attorney to deposit the check into her office account, making option I an incorrect choice. Either II or III would be an appropriate way for Attorney to proceed. Certainly option II satisfies the requirements of the Rules. Attorney has kept the funds separate from her own funds and is requesting payment from client. Option III is also appropriate, however. Model Rule 1.15, Comment [3] recognizes that lawyers often receive funds from which their fee is to be paid. So long as there isn't any dispute, a lawyer is not required to remit to the client funds that she reasonably believes represent fees. Further, it is acceptable for a lawyer to withdraw fees from a client trust account as they are earned. Therefore, by depositing the check in the client trust account and then writing separate check to herself and client, Attorney has fulfilled her obligation.

A is incorrect because it does not include III, which is also a correct choice.

B is incorrect because it does not include II, which is also a correct choice.

C is incorrect because it relies in part on I, which is incorrect and does not incorporate III, which is.

Question 49.

C is the correct answer. There is definitely a conflict of interest involved if Alpha represents Builder and Neighbor. A lawyer may not represent one client if it will be directly adverse to another client without the client's informed consent. Model Rule 1.7. This is true even if the lawyer would be acting as advocate against the client in a matter unrelated to the one in which the lawyer represents the client. Model Rule 1.7, Comment [6]. It is possible Alpha could undertake the representation of Neighbor with informed written consent from Builder, but since that option is not offered, C remains the best answer.

A is incorrect. The conflict of interest rule speaks to a lawyer's loyalty to a client, so it doesn't matter whether there are common issues in the two matters. If Alpha represents Neighbor in opposing Builder's petition for rezoning, Builder would be likely to feel betrayed, which would be likely to damage Alpha and Builder's lawyer-client relationship and interfere with Alpha's representation of Builder in the contract suit.

B is incorrect for the same reasons that A is incorrect. Loyalty to the client is the issue, and again, it doesn't matter what types of proceedings are involved.

D is incorrect. The issue is dealing with a concurrent conflict; what might or might not happen in the future has nothing to do with Alpha's decision whether it is proper to undertake representation of Neighbor.

Question 50.

A is the correct answer. With regard to *civil cases* the adversary system contemplates that the evidence in a case is to be marshaled competitively by the parties. Model Rule 3.4, Comment [1]. Likewise, a lawyer's duty not to conceal evidence in a civil case does not carry with it a duty to report or volunteer all relevant information. Annotations, *ABA Modal Rules of Professional Conduct*, Model Rule 3.4. Prosecutors, however, have special responsibilities. Model Rule 3.8. "A prosecutor has the responsibility of a minister of justice and not simply that of an advocate" (Model Rule 3.8, Comment [1]) and as such, "must make timely closure to the defense of all evidence or information known to the prosecutor that tends to negate the guilt of accused..."Model Rule 3.8(d). The fact that the girls' descriptions varied significantly at one point, but later matched almost perfectly raises a definite question as to the accuracy of their identification and "tends to negate the guilt" of Deft. Pros has a duty to reveal the existence of the tape to Deft's counsel.

B is incorrect. What Pros believes is not the point. If there is evidence or information that would raise a question as to the guilt of Deft, Pros must disclose the existence of that information or evidence in a timely manner.

C is incorrect. This is a true statement with regard to civil cases. See Model Rule 3.4. As discussed above, in a criminal case, a prosecutor has special responsibilities Model Rule 3.8.

D is incorrect. Pros responsibilities under Model Rule 3.8 exist independently of an request by defense counsel. The prosecutor's responsibility "carries with it specific obligations to see...that guilt is decided upon the basis of sufficient evidence." Model Rule 3.8, Comment [1].

Part Three
Sample NCBE Practice Questions

In Part Two, we offered our Model Answers to fifty of the Model Questions contained in the booklet **MPRE Sample Questions VI**, published by the National Conference of Bar Examiners. In Part Three, we reproduce verbatim additional questions contained in the NCBE booklet.

You're completely on your own now. Read each question carefully and circle the answer you think is the correct answer. Then check your answer against the NCBE Answer Key on page 173.

If you selected the right answer, try to articulate the reasons which lead you to that answer. Especially, write down which of the rules in the Model Code or the CJC you relied on in reasoning your way to your answer.

If you selected one of the three wrong answers, you have some work to do. Ask yourself: Why am I wrong? What rule did I miss or forget? What did I miss in the facts? How do I avoid making this mistake again?

Remember, the examiners may be knowledgeable and crafty, but there are only so many fact patterns they can concoct. If you review and re-review these questions and your own answers, there's a good chance you'll recognize essentially the same facts and issues in the questions on your own MPRE exam.

A. Practice Questions

1.

Attorney, a sole practitioner, limits his practice to personal injury cases. Attorney regularly places an advertisement in local newspapers. The advertisement contains the following statement: "Practice limited to personal injury cases, including medical malpractice." After seeing one of Attorney's advertisements, Baker approached Attorney for representation in a medical malpractice case. After a 30-minute interview Attorney told Baker:

> "I'm sorry, but I am very busy and your case appears to be very complicated. I would be happy to refer you to another lawyer who regularly practices in that field and who may have more room in her schedule. You should see another lawyer promptly before the statute of limitations expires and you lose your right to bring the lawsuit."

Although Attorney did not charge Baker for the interview, Baker was upset at the waste of 30 minutes of her time. Baker did not contact another lawyer until eight months later, when she learned that the statute of limitations on her claim had expired six months after her interview with Attorney. In fact, Baker had a meritorious medical malpractice claim.

Is Attorney <u>subject to civil liability</u>?

A. Yes, because Attorney falsely advertised his availability for medical malpractice cases.

B. Yes, because Attorney did not advise Baker as to the date the statute of limitations would expire.

C. No, because Attorney did not violate any duty owed to Baker.

D. No, because Attorney offered to refer Baker to another medical malpractice lawyer.

2.

Alpha and Beta practiced law under the firm name of Alpha and Beta. When Beta died, Alpha did not change the firm name. Thereafter, Alpha entered into an arrangement with another attorney, Gamma. Gamma pays Alpha a certain sum each month for office space and use of Alpha's law library and for secretarial services, but Alpha and

Gamma each has his own clients, and neither participates in the representation of the other's clients or shares in fees paid. On the entrance to the suite of offices shared by Alpha and Gamma are the words "Law Firm of Alpha, Beta, and Gamma."

Is Alpha subject to discipline?

A. Yes, because Beta was deceased when Alpha made the arrangement with Gamma.

B. Yes, because Gamma is not a partner of Alpha.

C. No, because Alpha and Beta were partners at the time of Beta's death.

D. No, because Gamma is paying a share of the rent and office expenses.

3.

Attorney was employed as a lawyer by the state Environmental Control Commission (ECC) for ten years. During the last two years of her employment. Attorney spent most of her time in the preparation, trial, and appeal of a case involving the discharge by Deftco of industrial effluent into a river in the state. The judgment in the case, which is now final, contained a finding of a continuing and knowing discharge of a dangerous substance into a major stream by Deftco and assessed a penalty of $25,000.

The governing statute also provides for private actions for damages by persons injured by the discharge of the effluent.

Attorney recently left the employment of ECC and went into private practice. Three landowners have brought private damage actions against Deftco. They claim their truck farms were contaminated because they irrigated them with water that contained effluent from dangerous chemicals discharged by Deftco. Deftco has asked Attorney to represent it in defense of the three pending actions.

Is Attorney subject to discipline if she represents Deftco in these actions?

A. Yes, unless the judgment in the prior case is determinative of Deftco's liability.

B. Yes, because Attorney had substantial responsibility in the matter while employed by ECC.

C. No, because Attorney has acquired special competence in the matter.

D. No, if all information acquired by Attorney while representing ECC is now a matter of public record.

4.

Attorney Alpha is skilled in trying personal injury cases. Alpha accepted the representation of Plaintiff in a personal injury case on a contingent fee basis. While preparing the case for trial, Alpha realized that the direct examination and cross-examination of the medical experts would involve medical issues with which Alpha was not familiar and, as a consequence, Alpha might not be able to represent Plaintiff competently.

Without informing Plaintiff, Alpha consulted Beta, who is both a lawyer and a medical doctor and who is a recognized specialist in the care and treatment of injuries of the type sustained by Plaintiff. Alpha and Beta agreed that Beta would participate in the trial to the limited extent of conducting the direct examination and cross-examination of the medical experts and that Alpha would divide the fee in proportion to the services performed and the responsibility assumed by each.

Was the arrangement between Alpha and Beta proper?

A. Yes, because the fee to be paid by Plaintiff was not increased by reason of Beta's association.

B. Yes, because the fee would be divided in proportion to the services performed and the responsibility assumed by each.

C. No, because Plaintiff was not advised of the association of Beta.

D. No, unless, upon conclusion of the matter, Alpha provides Plaintiff with a written statement setting forth the method of determining both the fee and the division of the fee with Beta.

5.

Attorney represents Client, a famous politician, in an action against Newspaper for libel. The case has attracted much publicity, and a jury trial has been demanded. After one of the pretrial hearings, as Attorney left the courthouse, news reporters interviewed Attorney. In responding to questions, Attorney truthfully stated:

> "The judge has upheld our right to subpoena the reporter involved, identified in our motion as Repo, and question her on her mental impressions when she prepared the article."

Is Attorney <u>subject to discipline</u> for making this statement?

A. Yes, because Attorney identified a prospective witness in the case.

B. Yes, because prospective jurors might learn of Attorney's remarks.

C. No, because the statement relates to a matter of public record.

D. No, because the trial has not commenced.

6.

Attorney Alpha has been employed as an assistant prosecutor in the district attorney's office during the time that an investigation of Deft was being conducted by that office. Alpha took no part in the investigation and had no knowledge of the facts other than those disclosed in the press. Two months ago, Alpha left the district attorney's office and formed a partnership with Attorney Beta.

Last week, Deft was indicted for offenses allegedly disclosed by the prior investigation. Deft asked Alpha to represent him. Alpha declined to do so, but suggested Beta.

Is Beta <u>subject to discipline</u> if Beta represents Deft?

A. Yes, because Alpha was employed in the district attorney's office while the investigation of Deft was being conducted.

B. Yes, unless the district attorney's office is promptly notified and consents to the representation.

C. No, unless Alpha participates in the representation or shares in the fee.

D. No, because Alpha had no responsibility for or knowledge of the facts of the investigation of Deft.

7.

Deft was on trial for the murder of Victim, who was killed during a barroom brawl. In the course of closing arguments to the jury, Prosecutor said,

> "Deft's whole defense is based on the testimony of Wit, who said that Victim attacked Deft with a knife before Deft struck him. No other witness testified to such an attack by Victim. I don't believe Wit was telling the truth, and I don't think you believe him either."

Was Prosecutor's statement <u>proper</u>?

A. Yes, if Prosecutor accurately stated the testimony in the case.

B. Yes, if Prosecutor, in fact, believed Wit was lying.

C. No, because Prosecutor alluded to the beliefs of the jurors.

D. No, because Prosecutor asserted his personal opinion about Wit's credibility.

8.

Attorney represents Client, plaintiff in a civil action that was filed a year ago and is about to be set for trial. Client informed Attorney that he could be available at any time during the months of October, November, and December. In discussing possible trial dates with opposing counsel and the court clerk, Attorney was advised that a trial date on October 5 was available and that the next available trial date would be December 10. Without first consulting Client, Attorney requested the December 10 trial date because she was representing Deft, the defendant in a felony criminal trial that was set for October 20 and she wanted as much time as possible to prepare for that trial.

Was it <u>proper</u> for Attorney to agree to the December trial date without obtaining Client's consent?

A. Yes, unless Client will be prejudiced by the delay.

B. Yes, because a criminal trial takes precedence over a civil trial.

C. No, because Attorney should manage her calendar so that her cases can be tried promptly.

D. No, unless Attorney was court-appointed counsel in the criminal case.

9.

Able, Baker, and Carter had been indicted for the armed robbery of the cashier of a grocery store. Together, Able and Baker met with Attorney and asked Attorney to represent them. Attorney then interviewed Able and Baker separately. Each told Attorney that the robbery had been committed by Carter while Able and Baker sat in Carter's car outside the store, that Carter had said he needed some cigarettes, and that each knew nothing of Carter's plan to rob the cashier. Attorney agreed to represent both Able and Baker. One week prior to the trial date, Able told Attorney that he wanted to plea bargain and that he was prepared to turn state's evidence and testify that Baker had loaned Carter the gun Carter used in the robbery. Able also said that he and Baker had shared in the proceeds of the robbery with Carter.

It is <u>proper</u> for Attorney to:

A. request court approval to withdraw as lawyer for both Able and Baker.

B. continue to represent Baker and, with Able's consent and court approval, withdraw as Able's lawyer.

C. continue to represent Able and, with Baker's consent and court approval, withdraw as Baker's lawyer.

D. continue to represent Able and Baker, but not call Able as a witness.

10.

While presiding over the trial of a highly publicized antitrust case, ABCO v. DEFO, Judge received in the mail a lengthy letter from Attorney, a local lawyer. The letter discussed the law applicable to ABCO v. DEFO. Judge knew that Attorney did not represent either party. Judge read the letter and, without mentioning its receipt to the lawyers in the pending case, filed the letter in his general file on anti-trust litigation.

Later, after reading the trial briefs in ABCO v. DUO, Judge concluded that Attorney's letter better explained the law applicable to the case pending before him than either of the trial briefs. Judge followed Attorney's reasoning in formulating his decision.

Was it <u>proper</u> for Judge to consider Attorney's letter?

A. Yes, because Judge did not initiate the communication with Attorney.

B. Yes, if Attorney did not represent any client whose interests could be affected by the outcome.

C. No, unless Judge, prior to rendering his decision, communicated its contents to all counsel and gave them an opportunity to respond.

D. No, because Attorney is not of record as counsel in the case.

11.

Attorney's recorded radio advertisement stated:

"For a fee of $600 Attorney will represent a party to a divorce that does not result in a court trial of a contested issue of fact."

Attorney had the advertisement prerecorded and approved by the appropriate bar agency for broadcast. Attorney retained a recording of the actual transmission in her office. Client, who had previously agreed with her husband to an uncontested dissolution of their marriage, heard the broadcast and called on Attorney in Attorney's office. Client told Attorney that she had heard the broadcast and asked Attorney to represent her. Attorney agreed to represent Client. Because of the nature of the parties' property, Attorney spent more time on the tax aspects of the case than Attorney anticipated. The time expended by Attorney, if charged at a reasonable hourly rate, would have resulted in a fee of $2,000. After the decree was entered, Attorney billed Client for $2,000.

Is Attorney subject to discipline?

A. No, because Attorney's fee was a reasonable charge for the time expended.

B. No, because Attorney, when the representation was accepted, did not anticipate the tax problems.

C. Yes, unless Client pays the fee without protest.

D. Yes, because Attorney charged a fee in excess of the advertised fee.

12.

Acton, a certified public accountant, has proposed to Attorney, a recognized specialist in the field of tax law, that Acton and Attorney form a partnership for the purpose of providing clients with tax-related legal and accounting services. Both Acton and Attorney have deserved reputations of being competent, honest, and trustworthy. Acton further proposes that the announcement of the proposed partnership, the firm stationery, and all public directory listings clearly state that Acton is a certified public accountant and that Attorney is a lawyer.

Is Attorney subject to discipline if he enters into the proposed partnership with Acton?

A. Yes, because one of the activities of the partnership would be providing legal services to clients.

B. Yes, because Attorney would be receiving fees paid for other than legal services.

C. No, because the partnership will assure to the public high-quality services in the fields of tax law and accounting.

D. No, if Attorney is the only person in the partnership who gives advice on legal matters.

13.

Client, who is under indictment for homicide, is represented by Attorney. In the course of representation, Client told Attorney that Client had previously killed two other persons in homicides completely unrelated to the murder indictment for which Attorney was providing representation. Attorney, with Client's consent, made a tape recording of Client's confession regarding the unrelated homicides. At Attorney's request, Client also drew a map on which he designated the remote locations of the graves of the victims of the unrelated killings. Those bodies have not been found by the police, and Client is not a suspect in either crime, both of which remain unsolved.

Is Attorney <u>subject to discipline</u> for failing to disclose voluntarily to the authorities his knowledge of the two prior murders and the locations of the bodies of the victims?

A. Yes, because, as an officer of the court, Attorney must disclose any knowledge that he has, whether privileged or not, concerning the commission of the prior crimes by Client.

B. Yes, because Attorney is impeding the state's access to significant evidence.

C. No, because Attorney did not represent or advise Client with respect to the prior crimes.

D. No, because the information was obtained by Attorney in the course of the representation.

14.

Attorney Alpha is recognized as an expert in securities regulation law. Corp, a corporation, retained Alpha's law firm to qualify Corp's stock for public sale. After accepting the matter, Alpha decided that he preferred to spend his time on cases with a larger fee potential, so he assigned responsibility for the Corp matter to Attorney Beta, an associate in Alpha's office who had recently been admitted to the bar.

Beta protested to Alpha that he, Beta, knew nothing about securities regulation law and that he had too little time to prepare himself to handle the Corp matter competently without substantial help from Alpha.

Alpha responded, "I don't have time to help you. Everyone has to start somewhere." Alpha directed Beta to proceed.

Was Alpha's conduct <u>proper</u> in this matter?

A. Yes, because as a member of the bar, Beta is licensed to handle any legal matter.

B. Yes, because Alpha may withdraw from a case if work on it would cause him unreasonable financial hardship.

C. No, because Alpha knew Beta was not competent to handle the matter, and Alpha failed to provide supervision adequate to protect the client's interest.

D. No, because Corp had not given Alpha permission to assign Beta to work on the matter.

15.

Attorney represents Bank in its commercial loan transactions. Corp has applied to Bank for a loan of $900,000 to be secured by a lien on Corp's inventory. The inventory, consisting of small items, constantly turns over. The security documents are complex and if improperly drawn could result in an invalid lien. Bank has approved the loan on the condition that Attorney prepare the necessary security instruments and that Corp pay Attorney's fees. This arrangement is customary in the city in which Attorney's law office and Bank are located. It is obvious to Attorney that he can adequately represent the interests of both Corp and Bank. After Corp and Bank consulted with other lawyers, each consented in writing to the representation.

Is it <u>proper</u> for Attorney to prepare the security documents under these circumstances?

A. Yes, because Bank and Corp have given their informed consent to the arrangement.

B. Yes, because the arrangement is customary in the community.

C. No, because Attorney's fees are being paid by Corp not Bank.

D. No, because Corp and Bank have differing interests.

16.

Attorney represented Plaintiff in Plaintiff's action for defamation against Defendant. After Defendant's lawyer had filed and served an answer, Attorney, at Plaintiff's direction, hired Inv, a licensed private investigator, and instructed Inv to attempt to interview Defendant without revealing his employment. Inv succeeded in interviewing Defendant privately and obtained an admission from Defendant that the statements Defendant had made were based solely on unsubstantiated gossip.

Is Attorney <u>subject to discipline</u> for obtaining the statement from Defendant in this matter?

A. No, because Attorney was following Plaintiff's instructions.

B. No, because the statement obtained was evidence that Defendant's allegations were unfounded.

C. Yes, because Attorney should have interviewed Defendant personally.

D. Yes, because Attorney instructed Inv to interview Defendant.

17.

Attorney represents Driver, the plaintiff in an automobile accident case. Two weeks before the date set for trial, Attorney discovered that Witt was an eyewitness to the accident. Attorney interviewed Witt. Witt's version of the accident was contrary to that of Driver and, if believed by the trier of fact, would establish that Driver was at fault. Witt told Attorney that she had not been interviewed by defense counsel.

Witt also told Attorney that she intended to leave for Europe the following week for a month's vacation unless she had an obligation to remain and attend the trial.

Attorney told Witt:

> "No one has subpoenaed you yet. You have no legal duty to make yourself available. Trials can be difficult affairs. Witnesses sometimes get very nervous because of the questions asked by the lawyers. Why don't you take the vacation as planned, and, by the time you return, the trial will be over."

Is Attorney <u>subject to discipline?</u>

A. Yes, because Attorney advised Witt to leave the jurisdiction.

B. Yes, because Attorney did not subpoena Witt knowing she was an eyewitness.

C. No, because Witt had not been subpoenaed by the defense.

D. No, because Attorney did not offer Witt any inducement not to appear at the trial.

18.

Judge, prior to her appointment to the probate court, was a partner in Law Firm. Law Firm had an extensive probate practice. At the time of Judge's appointment, Law Firm had pending before the court to which Judge was appointed numerous matters in which requests were being made for allowances for attorney's fees. When Judge left Law Firm, she was paid a cash settlement. She has no further financial interest in any matter handled by Law Firm. Judge is now being asked to rule on these requests for allowances for attorney's fees.

Is it <u>proper</u> for Judge to rule on these requests?

A. Yes, because Judge has no financial interest in the outcome of these cases.

B. Yes, if these requests are not contested.

C. No, unless Judge notes on the record in each case her prior association with Law Firm.

D. No, because Judge was associated with Law Firm when these matters were pending.

19.

Attorney, representing Client, with Client's approval settled a claim against Defendant for $60,000. The settlement agreement provided that one-half would be paid by Insco, Defendant's primary insurance carrier, and one-half by Sureco, a co-insurer. Attorney's agreed fee was 30% of the amount of the settlement. Attorney received Insco's check for $30,000 and a letter from Sureco advising that its check would be sent in two weeks. Attorney promptly advised Client and deposited the $30,000 in her Client Trust Account. Client demanded that Attorney send him the entire $30,000 and take her fee out of the funds to be received from Sureco.

Which of the following would now be <u>proper</u> for Attorney?

I. Send Client $30,000.

II. Send Client $21,000 and retain $9,000 in her Client Trust Account.

III. Send Client $21,000 and transfer $9,000 to her personal account.

A. I only

B. I and II, but not III

C. I and III, but not II

D. I, II, and III

20.

Attorney is a well-known tax lawyer and author. During congressional hearings on tax reform, Attorney testified to her personal belief and expert opinion on the pending reform package. She failed to disclose in her testimony that she was being paid well by a private client for her appearance. In her testimony, Attorney took the position favored by her client, but the position was one that Attorney believed was in the public interest.

Was it <u>proper</u> for Attorney to present this testimony without identifying her private client?

A. Yes, because Attorney conscientiously believed that the position she advocated before Congress was in the public interest.

B. Yes, because Congress is interested in the content of testimony and not in who is paying the witness.

C. No, because a lawyer may not accept a fee for trying to influence legislative action.

D. No, because a lawyer who appears in a legislative hearing should identify the capacity in which the lawyer appears.

21.

Attorney represented Baker in a claim involving a breach of Baker's employment contract. The case was settled without suit being filed. The proceeds of the settlement were paid directly to Baker, who subsequently paid Attorney in full for Attorney's fee and expenses. Thereafter, Attorney did no other work for Baker.

Baker is now being audited by the Internal Revenue Service (IRS). The IRS has asked Attorney for details of the settlement, including the amount claimed for each item of damage and the amounts paid for the items. Attorney reported the request to Baker who told Attorney not to provide the information to the IRS.

Is it <u>proper</u> for Attorney to furnish the information to the IRS?

A. Yes, if the information does not involve Attorney's work product.

B. Yes, because Attorney no longer represents Baker.

C. No, because Baker told Attorney not to provide the information.

D. No, unless Attorney believes the disclosure would be beneficial to Baker.

22.

Attorney and Broker, a licensed real estate broker, entered into an agreement whereby Broker was to recommend Attorney to any customer of Broker who needed legal services, and Attorney was to recommend Broker to any client of Attorney who wished to buy or sell real estate. Attorney's practice is limited almost entirely to real estate law.

Is Attorney subject to discipline for entering into the agreement with Broker?

A. Yes, because Attorney is compensating Broker for recommending Attorney's legal services.

B. Yes, because the arrangement constitutes the practice of law in association with a nonlawyer.

C. No, if neither Attorney nor Broker shares in the other's fees.

D. No, if the fees of Attorney and Broker do not clearly exceed reasonable fees for the services rendered by each.

23.

Attorney is employed by Client, a fugitive from justice under indictment for armed robbery. Attorney, after thorough legal research and investigation of the facts furnished by Client, reasonably believes the indictment is fatally defective and should be dismissed as a matter of law. Attorney advised Client of his opinion and urged Client to surrender. Client told Attorney that she would not surrender.

Attorney informed the district attorney that he represented Client and that he counseled Client to surrender, but that Client refused to follow his advice. Attorney has not advised Client on how to avoid arrest and prosecution and does not know where Client is hiding.

Is Attorney subject to discipline if he continues to represent Client?

A. Yes, because Client is engaged in continuing illegal conduct.

B. Yes, because Client refused to accept Attorney's advice and surrender.

C. No, because Attorney is not counseling Client to avoid arrest and prosecution.

D. No, because Attorney reasonably believes the indictment is defective.

24.

Attorney in his capacity as part-time assistant county attorney represented County in a criminal non-support proceeding against Husband. This proceeding concluded with an order directing Husband to pay or be jailed. Husband refused to pay.

Attorney, pursuant to applicable rules, is permitted to maintain a private law practice. Wife has discovered some assets of Husband. Attorney now has accepted employment from Wife to maintain a civil action against Husband to recover out of those assets arrearages due to Wife under Wife's support decree. Attorney did not obtain consent from the county attorney or from Husband to represent Wife in the civil action.

Is Attorney subject to discipline for accepting employment in Wife's civil action against Husband?

A. Yes, because Attorney did not obtain Husband's consent to the representation.

B. Yes, because Attorney had personal and substantial responsibility in the first proceeding.

C. No, because Attorneys responsibility in his public employment has terminated.

D. No, because Attorney is representing Wife's interest in both the criminal and the civil proceedings.

25.

Attorney is a lawyer for City and advises City on all tort claims filed against it. Attorney's advice is limited to recommending settlement and the amount thereof. If a claim is not settled and suit is filed, defense of the suit is handled either by lawyers for City's insurance carrier or by outside counsel specially retained for that purpose. In connection with any notice of claim and before suit is filed, Attorney arranges for an investigator to call upon the claimant at the claimant's home and, with no one else present, to interview the claimant and endeavor to obtain a signed statement of the claimant's version of the facts.

Claimant has filed a notice of claim against City. Attorney has sent an investigator to interview Claimant.

Is Attorney <u>subject to discipline</u> for arranging an interview with Claimant?

A. Yes, if Claimant was known by Attorney to be represented by counsel.

B. Yes, if the statement taken is later used to Claimant's disadvantage.

C. No, because Claimant had not filed suit at the time of the interview.

D. No, because Attorney would not be representing City in any subsequent litigation on Claimant's claim.

26.

Delta, a lawyer, has just joined the Law Offices of Alpha and Beta, a professional corporation engaged solely in the practice of law. Delta is a salaried associate and is not a member or shareholder of the professional corporation. Alpha's spouse, Veep, who is not a lawyer, is vice-president of the corporation and office manager. All of the other officers are lawyers in the firm. All of the corporate shares are held by lawyers in the corporation, except for ten shares held by the executor under the will of a lawyer-member who died one month previously and whose will is now being probated. Delta knows that Veep is an officer and not a lawyer.

Is Delta <u>subject to discipline</u>?

A. Yes, because Veep is an officer of the corporation.

B. Yes, if a nonlawyer holds the stock as the executor of the will of the deceased member.

C. No, because Delta is a salaried employee and not a member or shareholder of the corporation.

D. No, if Veep does not participate in any decision regarding a client or a client's case.

27.

Attorney is representing Plaintiff in a paternity suit against Defendant. Both Plaintiff and Defendant are well-known public figures, and the suit has attracted much publicity. Attorney has been billing Plaintiff at an agreed hourly fee for his services. Recently, Plaintiff told Attorney,

> "I'm going broke paying you. Why don't you let me assign you all media rights to books, movies, or television programs based on my suit as full payment for all services you will render me between now and the conclusion of the suit?"

Attorney replied,

> "I'll consider it, but first you should seek independent advice about whether such an arrangement is in your own best interests. Why don't you do so and call me next week."

Is Attorney <u>subject to discipline</u> if he agrees to Plaintiff's offer?

A. Yes, because the amount received by Attorney would be contingent on the receipts from the sale of media rights.
B. Yes, because Attorney has not concluded the representation of Plaintiff.
C. No, because the paternity suit is a civil and not a criminal matter.
D. No, if Plaintiff received independent advice before entering into the agreement.

28.

Four years ago, Attorney represented Husband and Wife, both high school teachers, in the purchase of a new home. Since then, Attorney prepared their tax returns and drafted their Wills.

Recently, Husband called Attorney and told her that he and Wife had decided to divorce, but wanted the matter to be resolved amicably. Husband stated that they were planning to file and process their own divorce case, utilizing the state's new streamlined divorce procedure, applicable in "no-fault" cases where there are no minor children. Husband asked if Attorney would agree to work with them to prepare a financial settlement agreement that could be presented to the divorce court, reminding Attorney that the couple's assets were modest and that they wanted to "split it all down the middle."

After considering the risks of a conflict of interest arising in this limited representation, Attorney wrote to the couple separately, and advised each that he or she might be better off with separate lawyers, but that Attorney would assist with the financial settlement agreement, charging an hourly fee of $140 per hour, provided that they were in complete agreement and remained so. Attorney advised that if a conflict developed, or if either party was dissatisfied or uncomfortable about continuing with the joint representation, Attorney would withdraw and would not represent either party from that point forward, forcing them to start all over again with separate lawyers. Finally, Attorney cautioned Husband and Wife that Attorney would be representing both of them equally, would not and could not favor one or the other, and that their separate communications to her could not be kept confidential from the other party. Both Husband and Wife signed their individual copy of the letter, consenting to the joint representation, and returned them to Attorney.

Was it proper for Attorney to accept the representation on these terms?

A. Yes, because there was little risk that the interests of either Husband or Wife would be materially prejudiced if no settlement was reached.

B. Yes, because Attorney had previously represented Husband and Wife in their joint affairs.

C. No, because Attorney conditioned representation upon receiving a waiver of client confidentially.

D. No, unless Attorney advised both Husband and Wife, in writing, that they should seek independent counsel before agreeing to enter into the financial settlement on the terms proposed.

29.

Attorney represented Client in negotiating a large real estate transaction. Buyer, who purchased the real estate from Client, has filed suit against both Client and Attorney, alleging fraud and violation of the state unfair trade practices statute. Attorney had advised Client by letter against making the statements relied on by Buyer as the basis for Buyer's claim. Attorney and Client are each represented by separate counsel. In responding to a deposition under subpoena, Attorney wishes to reveal, to the extent Attorney reasonably believes necessary to defend herself, confidential information imparted to Attorney by Client that will be favorable to Attorney but damaging to Client.

Is it proper for Attorney to reveal such information?

A. Yes, unless Client objects to the disclosure.

B. Yes, because Attorney may reveal such information to defend herself against a civil claim.

C. No, unless criminal charges have also been brought against Attorney.

D. No, because the disclosure will be detrimental to Client.

30.

Attorney, who is corporate counsel for Company, is investigating a possible theft ring in the parts department of Company. Attorney knows that Employee has worked in the parts department a long time and believes that Employee is a suspect in the thefts. Attorney believes that if Employee were questioned, Employee would not answer truthfully if she knew the real purpose of the questions. Attorney plans to question Employee and falsely tell her that she is not a suspect and that her answers to the questions will be held in confidence.

Is Attorney <u>subject to discipline</u> if she so questions Employee?

A. Yes, because Attorney's conduct involves misrepresentation.

B. Yes, unless Attorney first advises Employee to obtain counsel to represent Employee.

C. No, because no legal proceedings are now pending.

D. No, because Attorney did not give legal advice to Employee.

31.

Manufacturer sued Partco for Partco's breach of warranty regarding machine components furnished by Partco. Judge, who presided at the nonjury trial, sent Clerk, her law clerk, to Manufacturer's plant to observe the machine that was malfunctioning due to the allegedly defective parts. Clerk returned and told Judge that the machine was indeed malfunctioning and that Engineer, an employee of Manufacturer, had explained to Clerk how the parts delivered by Partco caused the malfunction. There was testimony at the trial that supported what Clerk learned on his visit. Judge rendered a judgment for Manufacturer.

Was Judge's conduct <u>proper</u>?

A. Yes, because Judge's judgment was supported by evidence at the trial.

B. Yes, because Judge has the right to gather facts concerning the trial.

C. No, because Judge has engaged in ex parte contacts that might influence the outcome of litigation.

D. No, unless Engineer was a witness at the trial and subject to cross-examination by Partco.

32.

Attorney regularly represented Client. When Client planned to leave on a world tour, Client delivered to Attorney sufficient money to pay Client's property taxes when they became due. Attorney placed the money in Attorney's Clients' Trust Account. When the tax payment date arrived, Attorney was in need of a temporary loan to close the purchase of a new personal residence. Because the penalty for late payment of taxes was only 2% while the rate for a personal loan was 6%, Attorney withdrew Client's funds from the Clients' Trust Account to cover Attorney's personal check for the closing. Attorney was confident that Client would not object. Ten days later, after the receipt of a large fee previously earned, Attorney paid Client's property taxes and the 2% penalty, fully satisfying Client's tax obligation. After Client returned, Attorney told Client what Attorney had done, and Client approved Attorney's conduct.

Is Attorney <u>subject to discipline</u>?

A. Yes, because Attorney failed to pay Client the ten days of interest at the fair market rate.

B. Yes, because Attorney used Client's funds for a personal purpose.

C. No, because Client was not harmed and Attorney reasonably believed at the time Attorney withdraw the money that Client would not object.

D. No, because when Attorney told Client what he had done, Client approved Attorney's conduct.

33.

Attorney entered into a written retainer agreement with Deft, who was the defendant in a criminal case. Deft agreed in writing to transfer title to Deft's automobile to Attorney if Attorney successfully prevented

Deft from going to prison. Later, the charges against Deft were dismissed.

Is Attorney <u>subject to discipline</u> for entering into this retainer agreement?

A. Yes, because Attorney agreed to a fee contingent on the outcome of a criminal case.

B. Yes, because a lawyer may not acquire a proprietary interest in a client's property.

C. No, because the charges against Deft were dismissed.

D. No, because the retainer agreement is in writing.

34.

Attorney Alpha filed a complaint on behalf of Client against Agri, a corporation, alleging that Agri had breached a valid oral contract entered into on Agni's behalf by Pres, the president and chief executive officer of Agri, to sell Client certain merchandise for a specified price. Attorney Beta, representing Agri, has flied an answer denying the contract and asserting the statute of frauds as a defense.

Attorney Beta has given notice to Alpha that he will take the deposition of Pres on the grounds that Pres will be out of the country on the date the case is set for trial. Pres is not a shareholder of Agri. Alpha would like to interview Pres, prior to the taking of the deposition, in order better to prepare her cross-examination.

Is Alpha <u>subject to discipline</u> if she interviews Pres without Beta's knowledge and consent?

A. No, unless Pres will be personally liable to Agri for damages in the event judgment is rendered against Agri.

B. No, because Pres allegedly entered into the contract on behalf of Agri.

C. Yes, because Pres is being called as an adverse witness.

D. Yes, because Pres is the president of Agri.

35.

Attorney represents ten plaintiffs who were injured when a train operated by Railroad was derailed. Railroad has offered Attorney a $500,000 lump sum settlement for the ten plaintiffs. Attorney has determined a division of the $500,000 among the ten plaintiffs with the amount paid each plaintiff dependent on the nature and extent of that person's injuries. Attorney believes the division is fair to each plaintiff.

Railroad will not settle any of the claims unless all are settled. Attorney has told each plaintiff the total amount Railroad is prepared to pay, the amount that the individual will receive, and the basis on which that amount was calculated. Attorney has not told any plaintiff the amount to be received by any other plaintiff. Attorney believes that if Attorney reveals to each plaintiff the amount of each settlement, there is danger that some plaintiffs will think that they are not getting enough in relation to the amounts others will receive and the entire settlement will be upset. Each of the plaintiffs has agreed to his or her settlement.

Is Attorney <u>subject to discipline</u> if Attorney effects such a settlement?

A. Yes, because Attorney is aiding the lawyer for Railroad in making a lump sum settlement.

B. Yes, because no individual plaintiff knows the amount to be received by any other plaintiff.

C. No, if to disclose all settlements to each plaintiff might jeopardize the entire settlement.

D. No, if the amount received by each plaintiff is fair and each plaintiff is satisfied.

36.

Attorney Alpha serves on a bar association committee established to counsel and rehabilitate lawyers who suffer from substance abuse. The day before Alpha was to leave on a fishing trip, Alpha's close friend, Attorney Beta, disclosed to Alpha that, over the preceding two years, Beta had become heavily addicted to cocaine and was afraid he had committed criminal offenses in his banking activities as a result of his addiction. Beta asked Alpha to represent him. Alpha agreed, but explained that Alpha could do little for two weeks and would consult with Beta immediately upon Alpha's return. While on the fishing trip, Cepa, an accountant who knew that Alpha represented Beta, told Alpha that Cepa had been retained by the trust department of Bank, a commercial bank, to audit several substantial trust accounts in which Bank and Beta are co-trustees. Cepa also told Alpha that the audit furnished incontrovertible proof that Beta had embezzled more than $100,000 from the trust accounts.

<u>Must</u> Alpha report Beta's embezzlement to the appropriate disciplinary authority?

A. Yes, because Alpha learned of Beta's embezzlement from Cepa.

B. Yes, because Alpha's failure to report would assist the concealment of Beta's breach of trust.

C. No, because Alpha gained the information while representing Beta.

D. No, because the information will probably be made public by Bank.

37.

The following advertisement appeared in a daily newspaper in a state in which both parties are members of the bar:

A. ALPHA, M.D., JD.

and

B. BETA, J.D.

Attorneys at Law

1000 "A" Street, City, State, 00000

Telephone (555) 555-5555

Are Alpha and Beta <u>subject to discipline</u>?

A. No, because both law and medicine are licensed professions.

B. No, if they possess the degree(s) stated.

C. Yes, because the reference to the M.D. degree is self-laudatory.

D. Yes, unless they limit their practice to areas in which a medical degree is relevant.

38.

While working on a complex matter for Client, Attorney Alpha, a partner in the law firm of Alpha and Beta, identified a particularly difficult issue of law that could prove decisive in the dispute. Alpha had not encountered this issue before and was uncertain of its effect. Alpha called Alpha's partner, Attorney Beta, and asked her for assistance.

Was it <u>proper</u> for Alpha to consult with Beta?

A. No, unless the total fee is not increased by the consultation.

B. No, because Client's consent was not previously obtained.

C. Yes, unless Alpha identified Client to Beta.

D. Yes, because Alpha and Beta are partners in the same firm.

39.

Judge, a state court judge, has presided over the pretrial proceedings in a case involving a novel contract question under the Uniform Commercial Code. During the pretrial proceedings, Judge has acquired considerable background knowledge of the facts and law of the matter and, therefore, is particularly well qualified to preside at the trial. Shortly before the trial date, Judge discovered that his brother owns a substantial block of stock in the defendant corporation. He determined that his brother's financial interests would be substantially affected by the outcome of the case. Although Judge believed he would be impartial, he disclosed to the parties, on the record, his brother's interest.

Is it <u>proper</u> for Judge to hear the case?

A. Yes, because Judge is particularly well qualified to preside at the trial.

B. Yes, because Judge believes his judgment will not be affected by his brother's stockholding.

C. No, because disqualification based on a relative's financial interest cannot be waived.

D. No, unless after proper proceedings in which Judge did not participate all parties and their lawyers consent in writing that Judge may hear the case.

40.

Attorney is representing Deft on a charge of armed robbery. Deft claims that the prosecution witness is mistaken in her identification. Deft has produced Baker, who will testify that Deft was in another city 500 miles away when the robbery occurred. Attorney knows that Baker is lying, but Deft insists that Baker be called on Deft's behalf.

Is Attorney <u>subject to discipline</u> if she calls Baker?

A. Yes, unless, before calling Baker, Attorney informs the court of her belief.

B. Yes, because Attorney knows Baker will be testifying falsely.

C. No, unless Attorney relies on the alibi defense in her argument before the jury.

D. No, because Deft has insisted that Baker be called as a witness on Deft's behalf.

41.

Attorney is a candidate for a judicial office that has been occupied by Incumbent for six years. Attorney has conducted a thorough investigation of Incumbent's personal and professional life.

Assume all factual statements are accurate. Which of the following statements is it proper for Attorney to make during the campaign?

I.   "Incumbent has been reversed by the appellate courts more than any other judge in the state during the preceding two years."

II.   "Incumbent was publicly censured by the state Judicial Qualification Commission on one occasion for his overbearing conduct in court."

III. "Incumbent was given a poor rating for judicial temperament in a county bar association poll."

IV.   "During the previous year, the average sentence in armed robbery cases tried in Incumbent's court was 3.5 years, and in murder cases was 8.2 years. If I am elected, I won't be soft on crime."

A. I only

B. I and II, but not III or IV

C. I, II, and III, but not IV

D. I, II, and IV, but not III

42.

The state bar association has offered Judge and her spouse free transportation and lodging to attend its institute on judicial reform. Judge is expected to deliver a banquet speech.

Is it proper for Judge to accept this offer?

A. Yes, unless the value of the transportation and lodging exceeds $500.

B. Yes, because the activity is devoted to the improvement of law.

C. No, if members of the bar association regularly appear in Judge's court.

D. No, because the bar association is offering free transportation to Judge's spouse.

43.

Attorney represents Client, a well-known contractor, before Agency, a state administrative agency. Agency has ordered Client to show cause why Client's license as a contractor should not be revoked for violation of agency regulations. In a newspaper interview prior to the administrative hearing, Attorney truthfully stated that:

I. "Client denies the charge made by Agency that Client engaged in conduct constituting grounds for revocation of Client's license as a contractor."

II. "The next step in the administrative process is the administrative hearing; if Agency is successful, we will appeal, and Agency still cannot revoke Client's license until a court affirms the finding for Agency."

III. "Client needs witnesses who are aware of the incidents that are the subject of the hearing."

Which of these statements would be proper?

A. I only

B. II only

C. III only

D. I, II, and III

44.

Leaving an airport, Attorney, who primarily practices criminal law, shared a cab with Doctor, a medical doctor. The cab was involved in a collision, and Doctor was seriously injured, while Attorney was only shaken up. Attorney accompanied Doctor to the hospital in the ambulance. Doctor believed that she was dying and asked Attorney to prepare a simple will for her. Attorney told Doctor, "I have never prepared a will, but hope that I can remember the basics from law school." Attorney then complied with Doctor's request. Doctor signed the will, and the two paramedics in the ambulance signed as witnesses.

Was it <u>proper</u> for Attorney to prepare the will?

A. Yes, unless Attorney omitted some required formality that rendered the will invalid.

B. Yes, because Attorney provided legal services that were reasonably necessary under the circumstances.

C. No, unless Doctor waived Attorney's malpractice liability.

D. No, because Attorney did not have the skill required for the representation.

45.

Attorney has recently started her own law firm with four other lawyers as associates. The law firm has moved into offices in a new building which is owned by Bank. Attorney has borrowed heavily from Bank to finance her new law firm. In addition, Bank provides the law firm with accounting services through its computer.

At Bank's suggestion, an employee of Bank, who is not a lawyer, serves as a part-time office manager for the law firm without compensation from the firm. The duties of the office manager are to advise the firm generally on fees and time charges, program matters for the computer services, and consult with Attorney on accounting and billing practices to ensure solvency.

Is the arrangement with Bank <u>proper</u>?

A. Yes, unless secrets or confidences of clients may be disclosed to Bank.

B. Yes, because the office manager is paid by Bank.

C. No, because a nonlawyer will be advising the law firm on fees and time charges.

D. No, because Bank will be involved in the practice of law.

46.

Attorney is representing Client, the plaintiff in a personal injury case, on a contingent fee basis. Client is without resources to pay for the expenses of the investigation and the medical examinations necessary to prepare for trial. Client asked Attorney to pay for these expenses. Attorney declined to advance the funds but offered to guarantee Client's promissory note to a local bank in order to secure the funds needed to cover those expenses. Client has agreed to reimburse Attorney in the event Attorney incurs liability on the guaranty.

Is Attorney <u>subject to discipline</u> if she guarantees Client's promissory note?

A. Yes, because Attorney is lending her credit to Client.

B. Yes, because Attorney is helping to finance litigation.

C. No, because the funds will be used for trial preparation.

D. No, because Attorney took the case on a contingent fee basis.

47.

Attorney Alpha represents Defendant in an action for personal injuries. Alpha, pursuant to Defendant's authorization, made an offer of settlement to Attorney Beta, who represents Plaintiff. Beta has not responded to the offer, and Alpha is convinced that Beta has not communicated the offer to Plaintiff. State law authorizes a defendant to move for a settlement conference and to tender an offer of settlement. If such a motion is made and the offer is rejected by Plaintiff and the eventual judgment does not exceed the amount of the offer, Plaintiff must bear all costs of litigation, including reasonable fees, as determined by the court, for Defendant's counsel.

Alpha, with Defendant's consent, filed a motion requesting a settlement conference, tendered an offer to settle for $25,000, and served copies of the motion and tender on Beta and on Plaintiff personally.

Is Alpha <u>subject to discipline</u> for serving Plaintiff with a copy of the motion and tender?

A. Yes, unless service of copies of the motion and tender on Plaintiff were authorized by statute or rule of court.

B. Yes, unless Alpha first informed Beta of Alpha's intention to serve copies of the motion and tender on Plaintiff.

C. No, because the decision to accept or reject a settlement offer rests with the client.

D. No, because the motion and tender became public documents when they were filed in court.

48.

Attorney Alpha represents Wife in a marriage dissolution proceeding that involves bitterly contested issues of property division and child custody. Husband is represented by Attorney Beta. After one day of trial, Husband, through Beta, made a settlement offer. Because of Husband's intense dislike for Alpha, the proposed settlement requires that Alpha agree not to represent Wife in any subsequent proceeding, brought by either party, to modify or enforce the provisions of the decree. Wife wants to accept the offer, and Alpha believes that the settlement offer made by Husband is better than any award Wife would get if the case went to judgment.

Is it proper for Alpha to agree that Alpha will not represent Wife in any subsequent proceeding?

A. Yes, because the restriction on Alpha is limited to subsequent proceedings in the same matter.

B. Yes, if Alpha believes that it is in Wife's best interests to accept the proposed settlement.

C. No, because the proposed settlement would restrict Alpha's right to represent Wife in the future.

D. No, unless Alpha believes that Wife's interests can be adequately protected by another lawyer in the future.

49.

Attorney represented Plaintiff, who was the plaintiff in litigation that was settled, with Plaintiff's approval, for $25,000. Attorney received a check in that amount from Defendant, payable to Attorney's order. Attorney endorsed and deposited the check in Attorney's Client Trust Account. Attorney promptly notified Plaintiff and billed Plaintiff $5,000 for legal fees. Plaintiff disputed the amount of the fee and wrote Attorney, stating, "I will agree to pay $3,000 as a reasonable fee for the work you did, but I will not pay anything more than that."

It is proper for Attorney to:

I. retain the entire $25,000 in Attorney's Client Trust Account until the fee dispute is settled.

II. send Plaintiff $20,000, transfer $3,000 to Attorney's office account, and retain $2,000 in Attorney's Client Trust Account until the dispute is settled.

III. send Plaintiff $20,000 and transfer $5,000 to Attorney's office account.

A. I only

B. II only

C. I and II, but not III

D. I, II, and III

50.

In Attorney's closing statement to the court in a bench trial, Attorney said,

> "Your honor, I drive on the street in question every day and I know that a driver cannot see cars backing out of driveways as the one did in this case. I believe that my client was not negligent, and I ask you to so find."

Was Attorney's closing argument <u>proper</u>?

A. Yes, if Attorney was speaking truthfully and not trying to deceive the court.

B. Yes, because the rules of evidence are very liberal when the trial is before a judge without a jury.

C. No, because Attorney asserted Attorney's personal knowledge of facts in issue.

D. No, if there is no other evidence in the record about the facts asserted by Attorney.

51.

Plaintiff, who is not a lawyer, is representing himself in small claims court in an action to recover his security deposit from his former landlord. Plaintiff told Attorney, a close friend who lived near him, about this case, but did not ask Attorney for any advice. Attorney said,

> "I'll give you some free advice. It would help your case if the new tenants would testify that the apartment was in good shape when they moved in, and, contrary to the allegations of your former landlord, it was not, in fact, repainted for them."

Plaintiff followed Attorney's advice and won his case.

Is Attorney <u>subject to discipline</u> for assisting Plaintiff in preparing for his court appearance?

A. Yes, because Attorney assisted Plaintiff in the practice of law.

B. Yes, because Attorney offered unsolicited, in-person legal advice.

C. No, because Plaintiff was representing himself in the proceedings.

D. No, because Attorney was not compensated for his advice.

52.

Attorney is defending Client, who has been indicted for burglary. During an interview, Client stated to Attorney that before he had consulted Attorney, Client had committed perjury while testifying before the grand jury that indicted him.

Attorney is <u>subject to discipline</u> if she:

A. continues to represent Client.

B. continues to represent Client unless Client admits his perjury.

C. does not inform the authorities of the perjury.

D. informs the authorities of the perjury.

53.

Attorney is employed in the legal department of Electco, a public utility company, and represents that company in litigation. Electco has been sued by a consumer group that alleges Electco is guilty of various acts in violation of its charter. Through its general counsel, Electco has instructed Attorney not to negotiate a settlement but to go to trial under any circumstances since a precedent needs to be established. Attorney believes the case should be settled if possible.

<u>Must</u> Attorney withdraw as counsel in the case?

A. Yes, if Electco is controlling Attorney's judgment in settling the case.

B. Yes, because a lawyer should endeavor to avoid litigation.

C. No, if Electco's defense can be supported by a good faith argument.

D. No, because as an employee, Attorney is bound by the instructions of the general counsel.

54.

Four years ago, Alpha was a judge in a state court of general jurisdiction and heard the civil case of Plaintiff against Defendant in which Plaintiff prevailed and secured a judgment for $50,000 which was sustained on appeal. Since then Alpha has resigned from the bench and returned to private practice. Defendant has filed suit to enjoin enforcement of the judgment on the grounds of extrinsic fraud in its procurement. Plaintiff has now asked Alpha to represent Plaintiff in defending the suit to enjoin enforcement.

Is it _proper_ for Alpha to accept the representation of Plaintiff in this matter?

A. Yes, because Alpha would be upholding the decision of the court.

B. Yes, if Alpha's conduct of the first trial will not be in issue.

C. No, unless Alpha believes the present suit is brought in bad faith.

D. No, because Alpha had acted in a judicial capacity on the merits of the original case.

55.

Attorney Alpha represents Plaintiff in a personal injury action against Defendant, who is represented by Attorney Beta. Alpha had heard that Defendant was anxious to settle the case and believed that Beta had not informed Defendant of a reasonable settlement offer made by Alpha. Alpha instructed Alpha's nonlawyer investigator, Inv, to tell Defendant about the settlement offer so Alpha could be sure that Beta does not force the case to trial merely to increase Beta's fee. Inv talked to Defendant as instructed.

Is Alpha _subject to discipline_?

A. Yes, because Defendant was represented by counsel.

B. Yes, because Alpha was assisting Inv in the unauthorized practice of law.

C. No, because Inv is not a lawyer.

D. No, if Alpha reasonably believed Beta was not keeping Defendant informed.

56.

Attorney served two four-year terms as the governor of State immediately prior to reopening his law office in State. Attorney printed and mailed an announcement of his return to private practice to members of the bar, persons who had previously been his clients, and personal friends whom he had never represented. The printed announcement stated that Attorney had reopened his law office, gave his address and telephone number, and added that he had been governor of State for the past eight years.

Is Attorney <u>subject to discipline</u> for the announcement?

A. Yes, because it was mailed to persons who had not been his clients.

B. Yes, because his service as governor is unrelated to his ability as a lawyer.

C. No, because the information in the announcement is true.

D. No, because all of the information was already in the public domain.

57.

Attorney placed Associate, recently admitted to the bar, in complete charge of the work of the paralegals in Attorney's office. That work consisted of searching titles to real property, an area in which Associate had no familiarity. Attorney instructed Associate to review the searches prepared by the paralegals, and thereafter to sign Attorney's name to the required certifications of title if Associate was satisfied that the search accurately reflected the condition of the title. This arrangement enabled Attorney to lower office operating expenses. Attorney told Associate that Associate should resolve any legal questions that might arise and not to bother Attorney because Attorney was too busy handling major litigation.

Is it <u>proper</u> for Attorney to assign Associate this responsibility?

A. Yes, if the paralegals are experienced in searching titles.

B. Yes, because Attorney is ultimately liable for the accuracy of the title searches.

C. No, unless it enables Attorney to charge lower fees for title certification.

D. No, because Attorney is not adequately supervising the work of Associate.

58.

The law firm of Able & Baker agreed to represent Client in various business matters. The written retainer agreement called for Client to pay Able & Baker's hourly rates of $180 per hour for a partner's time and $110 per hour for an associate's time. The representation proceeded, Able & Baker submitted monthly bills, which Client paid promptly, After two years, Able & Baker decided to increase their hourly rates by $10. Able & Baker thereafter billed Client at their new rates, but did not specifically inform Client of the increase. Client continued to pay monthly bills promptly.

Are Able & Baker subject to discipline?

A. Yes, because the entire original fee agreement was required to be in writing.

B. Yes, because Client did not consent to the increase.

C. No, if the $10 hourly increase is reasonable.

D. No, because Client agreed in writing to pay Able & Baker's hourly rate.

59.

During the closing argument to the jury in a civil tax fraud case, Attorney, representing the government, quoted a portion of Defendant's testimony and then said:

I. "The testimony of Defendant directly contradicts the testimony of two witnesses for the government."

II. "I ask you, who has the reason to lie, the two witnesses for the government or Defendant?"

III. "I can truthfully say I have never seen a witness less worthy of belief."

Which of the above statements by Attorney would be proper?

A. I only

B. I and II, but not III

C. II and III, but not I

D. I, II, and III

60.

Attorney's standard retainer contract in divorce cases provides for the payment of a fee of one-third of the amount of alimony or property settlement secured by Attorney. Attorney declines to represent clients who do not agree to this arrangement.

Is Attorney's standard retainer contract <u>proper</u>?

A. Yes, because clients often prefer to pay a lawyer a fee based on the outcome of the case.

B. Yes, if a fee of one-third is not excessive.

C. No, because a lawyer may not acquire a proprietary interest in a cause of action.

D. No, because the fee is contingent.

61.

Attorney Alpha was retained by Client to represent Client in defense of an action brought against Client by Plaintiff. In order to obtain ample time for settlement negotiations, Alpha immediately requested and obtained from opposing counsel, Attorney Beta, a stipulation extending Client's time to answer the complaint until ten days after receipt of written demand from Beta. Four months later, no settlement had been reached, and on May 1, Beta wrote Alpha demanding that an answer be filed within ten days. When no answer was filed by May 15, Beta had a default judgment entered in favor of Plaintiff.

Alpha was away on a two-month vacation when Beta's letter was received in her office. When Alpha returned on June 15, she promptly moved to have the default set aside and her motion was granted.

Is Alpha <u>subject to discipline</u>?

A. Yes, unless she makes restitution to Client for any loss sustained by Client.

B. Yes, if she did not make provision for the handling of her pending cases while she was away.

C. No, because the default judgment was set aside.

D. No, unless she knew that Beta had demanded that an answer be filed within ten days.

62.

Attorney represents Defendant, a prominent businessman, in a civil paternity suit brought by Plaintiff, who was formerly Defendant's employee. Blood tests did not exclude Defendant's paternity, and the case is being tried before a jury. The result turns on questions of fact. Defendant has steadfastly denied that he had sexual relations with Plaintiff, while Plaintiff has testified that they had sexual relations while on business trips and in her home. The trial has generated great public interest and is closely followed by the news media.

When Plaintiff completed her testimony, Attorney was interviewed by a newspaper reporter.

Which of the following statements, if believed by Attorney to be true, would be proper for Attorney to make?

I. "As stated in our pleadings, we expect to prove that other men could be the father of Plaintiff's child."

II. "We have scientific medical tests proving that Defendant is sterile."

III. "We have been unable to locate several people whose testimony will be helpful to us, and I implore them to contact me immediately."

A. II only.

B. III only.

C. I and III, but not II.

D. I, II, and III.

63.

Attorney Alpha is a lawyer running for election as a state judge. Attorney Beta, who practices law in the same community as Alpha, has frequently observed Alpha's courtroom demeanor in litigated cases. Based on those experiences. Beta believes that Alpha does not have a proper judicial temperament. A local news reporter asked Beta how Beta would rate the candidates, and Beta responded in good faith, "I think Alpha is unsuited for the bench. Alpha lacks the proper judicial temperament and would make a very poor judge." A local newspaper with a wide circulation quoted Beta's remarks.

Were Beta's remarks proper?

A. Yes, because Beta was not seeking judicial office.

B. Yes, because Beta believed Alpha was unsuited for the bench.

C. No, because the remarks serve to bring the judiciary into disrepute.

D. No, because a lawyer should not publicly comment on candidates for judicial office.

64.

Attorney has been representing Client in a matter in litigation. During protracted pretrial proceedings, Client complained bitterly about the time and expense involved and insisted that Attorney take steps to terminate the pretrial proceedings. Attorney believes that to do so would jeopardize Client's interests and has so informed Client. Attorney believes that the case cannot be adequately prepared for trial without further pretrial proceedings that will require an additional six months' delay and involve further expense. Client insists that Attorney forego any further pretrial proceedings and set the case for trial at the earliest available date. There are several other competent lawyers who are willing to undertake the representation.

Is it proper for Attorney to ask leave of the court to withdraw?

A. Yes, because a lawyer may discontinue representation in a civil case at any time before trial.

B. Yes, because Client's conduct makes it unreasonably difficult for Attorney to represent Client effectively and competently.

C. No, because Attorney must follow Client's instructions.

D. No, unless Client consents to Attorney's withdrawal.

65.

The judicial district in which Judge sits has a rule that allows litigants two postponements as a matter of right. After that, a litigant who moves for a postponement must convince the presiding judge that a postponement is appropriate. Judge routinely grants additional postponements because, in her view,

> "What harm is done if one of the litigants wants a postponement? The worst that can happen is that the parties have more time to negotiate and thus are more likely to settle."

Are Judge's actions proper?

A. Yes, because Judge is exercising her judicial discretion.

B. Yes, because a party objecting to a postponement can seek appellate review.

C. No, because judges have no official obligation to encourage private settlements.

D. No, because Judge should expedite the determination of matters before her.

66.

Two years ago, Attorney was employed by State's Department of Transportation (DOT) to search title to several tracts of land. Attorney has not been employed by DOT during the last year. Recently, DOT instituted proceedings to condemn a tract, owned by Owner, for a new highway route. Owner asked Attorney to represent her in obtaining the highest amount of compensation for the condemnation. Owner's tract is one of the tracts on which Attorney searched title two years ago. Attorney remembers that Engineer, a DOT engineer, once drafted a confidential memorandum advising against running a new highway across Owner's land because of potential adverse environmental impact. Because of this information, Attorney believes it is possible to prevent the condemnation of Owner's land or to increase the settlement amount.

It is proper for Attorney to:

A. represent Owner on the issue of damages only and not disclose the information that might prevent the condemnation.

B. represent Owner and attempt to prevent the condemnation by using the information about the adverse environmental impact.

C. refuse to represent Owner but disclose to Owner the information about the adverse environmental impact.

D. refuse to represent Owner and not disclose the information about the adverse environmental impact.

67.

Attorney, who had represented Testator for many years, prepared Testator's will and acted as one of the two subscribing witnesses to its execution. Testator's sister and brother were his sole heirs. The will left Testator's entire estate to his sister and nothing to his brother. Upon Testator's death two years later, Executor, the executor named in the will, asked Attorney to act as his lawyer in the probate of the will and the administration of the estate. At that time, Executor informed Attorney that Testator's brother would concede that the will was properly executed but intended to contest the will on the ground that he had been excluded because of fraud previously practiced on Testator by Testator's sister. The other subscribing witness to the will predeceased Testator, and Attorney will be called as a witness solely for the purpose of establishing the due execution of the will.

Is it <u>proper</u> for Attorney to accept the representation?

A. Yes, if there is no contested issue of fact with respect to the formal execution of the will.

B. Yes, because Executor has no beneficial interest under the will.

C. No, unless Attorney's services are necessary to avoid substantial hardship to Executor.

D. No, because Attorney will be called as a witness in the case.

68.

Attorney has been retained to defend an adult charged with a sex offense involving a minor. Attorney believes that, in order to win the case, she must keep parents of minor children off the jury. Attorney instructed her investigator as follows:

> "Visit the neighborhood of those prospective jurors on the panel with minor children. Ask the neighbors if they know of any kind of unusual sex activity of the prospective juror or any member of the family. This talk will get back to the prospective jurors, and they will think of excuses not to serve. But don't under any circumstances talk directly with any prospective juror or member of the family."

Is Attorney <u>subject to discipline</u> for so instructing her investigator?

A. Yes, unless the prospective jurors investigated are, in fact, selected to serve on the jury in the case.

B. Yes, because the investigation is intended to harass prospective jurors and members of their families.

C. No, if the matters inquired into might be relevant to a prospective juror's qualifications to serve in the case.

D. No, because no prospective juror was directly contacted.

69.

Client has retained Attorney to represent Client in a contract suit. Attorney's retainer agreement provided that Attorney's fees would be based on a fixed hourly rate, payable at the end of each calendar month. Two months before trial, Client fell behind in the payment of Attorney's monthly billing for fees. Attorney included the following statement on Attorney's last billing to Client:

> "Your account is more than thirty days past due. If amounts due are not paid promptly in accordance with our agreement, I will terminate the representation. If you cannot pay the amount due, I will accept an assignment of your cause of action as security for your fee to me."

Two weeks after the last billing, Attorney telephoned Client and told Client that Attorney would withdraw from representing Client if the bill was not paid within forty-eight hours or adequate security given for its payment.

If the bill remains unpaid or unsecured after forty-eight hours, it would be proper for Attorney to:

I.   upon notice to Client, move the court for permission to withdraw.

II. turn Client's file over to another experienced lawyer in town and notify Client that Attorney no longer represents Client.

III. accept an assignment of Client's cause of action as security for Attorney's fee.

A. I only

B. II only

C. I and II, but not III

D. I, II, and III

70.

Attorney represented Plaintiff in an action against several defendants. The retainer agreement provided that Plaintiff would pay all costs and expenses of litigation and would, on demand, reimburse Attorney for any costs or expenses advanced by Attorney. After serving process on two defendants, Attorney had difficulty locating and serving the remaining defendants. Plaintiff approved the hiring of an investigator to locate and serve the defendants, and Attorney advanced the costs for the investigator. When Attorney asked Plaintiff for reimbursement, Plaintiff refused to pay. Attorney then told Plaintiff that Attorney would do no more work on the case until Attorney was reimbursed for the amount advanced.

Thereafter, one of the defendants filed a counterclaim that required a responsive pleading within thirty days. Because Attorney had not been paid, Attorney permitted the time to respond to the counterclaim to expire without filing a responsive pleading, and a default was entered on the counterclaim. Later, Plaintiff reimbursed Attorney for the costs Attorney had advanced, and Attorney was successful in having the default on the counterclaim set aside. The case was tried, and Plaintiff prevailed on Plaintiff's complaint, and the counterclaimant recovered nothing.

Is Attorney <u>subject to discipline</u> for not initially filing a responsive pleading to the counterclaim?

A. Yes, because Attorney neglected Plaintiff's cause.

B. Yes, unless Attorney had asked leave of court to withdraw.

C. No, because Plaintiff breached the agreement to reimburse Attorney.

D. No, because Plaintiff did not sustain any prejudice as a result of Attorney's action.

71.

Judge, prior to her recent appointment to the federal court, had been an outspoken and effective opponent of the racial segregation policies of Gov, a foreign country's government. As part of its worldwide tour, Gov's national soccer team scheduled a soccer match with a team in this country. Several civil rights groups have applied to Judge for an order enjoining the playing of the proposed match. The matter is now pending. Only legal issues are presented. Judge, after painstaking consideration, has privately concluded that she cannot decide the legal questions without bias against the representatives of Gov's government. However, no one has made a motion to disqualify Judge.

<u>Must</u> Judge recuse herself in the pending matter?

A. Yes, unless Judge believes she has greater expertise than other judges on the court in legal issues involving racial segregation.

B. Yes, because Judge believes that she cannot be impartial.

C. No, because the only issues presented for decision are legal questions.

D. No, because none of the interested parties has moved to disqualify Judge.

72.

Client telephoned Attorney, who had previously represented Client. Client described a problem on which he needed advice and made an appointment for the following week to discuss the matter with Attorney. Prior to the appointment, Attorney performed 5 hours of preliminary research on Client's problem. At the end of the appointment, Client agreed that Attorney should pursue the matter, agreed to a fee of $100 per hour, and gave Attorney a check for $5,000 to cover the 5 hours already worked and as an advance on further fees and expenses.

Attorney gave the check to the office bookkeeper with the directions to "Deposit the check in the Clients' Trust Account and immediately transfer $3,000 to our General Office Account to cover the 5 hours of research already conducted plus the 25 additional hours I'll spend on it next week." At that time, Attorney reasonably believed that Attorney would spend 25 additional hours on the case.

The bookkeeper followed these directions. The next week, Attorney worked diligently on the matter for 23 hours. Reasonably believing that no significant work remained to be done on the matter, Attorney directed the bookkeeper to transfer $200 from the General Office Account to the Clients' Trust Account. Attorney then called Client and made an appointment to discuses the status of the matter.

Is Attorney <u>subject to discipline</u>?

A. Yes, because Attorney accepted legal fees in advance of performing the work.

B. Yes, because Attorney transferred funds for unearned fees to the General Office Account.

C. No, because Attorney transferred the $200 owed to Client from the General Office Account to the Clients' Trust Account.

D. No, because Attorney reasonably believed that Attorney would spend 25 additional hours on the case.

73.

Candidate, a member of the bar, is a candidate for judicial office in an election. Candidate personally asked several of his friends to contribute

$1,000 each to kick off his campaign. After Candidate's friends made the contributions, Candidate, who was elated by the support, formed a committee to collect more contributions. Candidate then turned over the contributions to the committee and began campaigning in earnest.

Is Candidate <u>subject to discipline</u>?

A. No, because Candidate turned over the funds to his committee.

B. No, unless the committee includes lawyers likely to practice before Candidate.

C. Yes, unless none of the original contributors was a lawyer.

D. Yes, because Candidate personally solicited funds.

74.

Judge Alpha has recently resigned from the state trial court bench. While she was a judge and supervising activity in cases pending before Judge Beta, who was on vacation, Alpha entered an administrative order changing the courtroom in which the case of Able v. Baker was to be tried. After trial and appeal, the case was remanded for a new trial. The plaintiff in Able v. Baker has now decided to change lawyers and has asked Alpha to try the case.

Will Alpha be <u>subject to discipline</u> if she tries this case on behalf of the plaintiff?

A. Yes, because Alpha acted officially as a judge with respect to an aspect of the case.

B. Yes, because Alpha would try the case before a judge of the court on which Alpha previously sat.

C. No, because Alpha did not act as a judge with respect to a substantial matter or on the merits of the case.

D. No, because any information that Alpha learned about the case while acting as a judge was a matter of public record.

75.

Although licensed to practice law in State, Attorney Alpha does not practice law but works as an investment broker. Alpha could have elected inactive status as a member of the bar, but chose not to do so. Recently, in connection with a sale of worthless securities, Alpha made materially false representations to Victim, an investment customer.

Victim sued Alpha for civil fraud, and a jury returned a verdict in Victim's favor. Alpha did not appeal.

Is Alpha subject to discipline?

A. Yes, because Alpha was pursuing a non-legal occupation while an active member of the bar.

B. Yes, because Alpha's conduct was fraudulent.

C. No, because Alpha was not convicted of a crime.

D. No, unless the standard of proof in State is the same in lawyer disciplinary cases and civil cases.

76.

Client was an experienced oil and gas developer. Client asked Attorney for representation in a suit to establish Client's ownership of certain oil and gas royalties. Client did not have available the necessary funds to pay Attorney's reasonable hourly rate for undertaking the case. Client proposed instead to pay Attorney an amount in cash equal to 20% of the value of the proceeds received from the first year royalties Client might recover as a result of the suit. Attorney accepted the proposal and took the case.

Is Attorney subject to discipline?

A. Yes, because the agreement gave Attorney a proprietary interest in Client's cause of action.

B. Yes, unless the fee Attorney receives does not exceed that which Attorney would have received by charging a reasonable hourly rate.

C. No, because Client rather than Attorney proposed the fee arrangement.

D. No, because Attorney may contract with Client for a reasonable contingent fee.

77.

Attorney has been hired by Client to represent Client in a civil commitment proceeding initiated by the state. Client is now undergoing psychiatric evaluation to determine whether civil commitment should be ordered. Client told Attorney that Client intends to commit suicide as soon as the tests are completed, and Attorney believes that Client will carry out this threat. Suicide and attempted suicide are crimes in the state.

Is it <u>proper</u> for Attorney to disclose Client's intentions to the authorities?

A. Yes, because the information concerns a future crime and is not protected by the attorney-client evidentiary privilege.

B. Yes, because the information concerns a future crime that is likely to result in Client's imminent death.

C. No, unless Attorney knows that Client has attempted suicide in the past.

D. No, because disclosure would aid the state in its civil commitment case against Client.

78.

Attorney is a long-time member of the state legislature and serves on the legislative budget committee that funds the local trial courts in the state. Attorney also maintains a part-time law practice as is permitted in the state. Able, an influential businessperson, who regularly makes significant contributions to Attorney's political campaigns, asked Attorney to help Able's uncle, Baker, who was involved in a bitter divorce. Attorney called the trial judge sitting on Baker's case, a personal friend of Attorney. In discussing some upcoming votes of the budget committee with the judge, Attorney mentioned that Baker was the type of solid citizen and influential person who could help garner support for the budget and thus ensure the economic health of the judicial system.

Is Attorney <u>subject to discipline</u>?

A. Yes, if the trial judge ruled in Baker's favor.

B. Yes, because Attorney used her public position to attempt to influence a tribunal in a pending matter.

C. No, if Attorney called the trial judge in her capacity as a legislator and not as Baker's lawyer.

D. No, because members of the state legislature are permitted by law to engage in part-time legal practice.

79.

Attorney agreed to represent Able, a client, in bringing a lawsuit. Attorney and Able executed Attorney's preprinted retainer form that provides, in part:

"The client agrees to pay promptly Attorney's fees for services. In addition, the client and Attorney agree to release each other from any and all liability arising from the representation. The client agrees that Attorney need not return the client's file prior to receiving the client's executed release. Attorney agrees to return the client's file promptly upon receipt of all fees owed and of the client's executed release."

During their initial meeting, Attorney recommended that Able consult independent counsel before signing the retainer agreement, but Able chose not to do so. Attorney reasonably believes that his fee is fair and that the quality of his work will be competent.

Is Attorney's retainer agreement with Able <u>proper</u>?

A. Yes, because Attorney furnished consideration by agreeing to release Able from liability and to return Able's files.

B. Yes, because Attorney reasonably believes that his fee is fair and that the quality of his work will be competent.

C. No, because Attorney is attempting to limit prospectively his liability for malpractice.

D. No, because Attorney uses a preprinted form for all retainers.

80.

Attorney represents Corp, a defendant in a product liability case. Engineer, a Corp employee nearing retirement, was likely to be a key witness in the case, as she had been in charge of all of Corp's product safety testing during the relevant period. Engineer had been very critical of Corp's safety testing procedures during that period and had repeatedly complained that the product at issue had not been adequately tested. Engineer's views were reduced to writing and were well known to many employees of Corp. Because of the early stage of the case, however, plaintiff's counsel was not yet aware of Engineer's existence or her views.

Aware of Engineer's views, Attorney approached Corp's officials and recommended that it offer Engineer a special package of severance benefits if she would retire immediately and move to the Bahamas. Attorney believed that if Engineer accepted this offer, she would be beyond the subpoena power of the court in which the suit against Corp was pending. Corp adopted Attorney's recommendation and made the offer. Engineer accepted it. Attorney did not disclose Engineer's identity to plaintiff's counsel.

Is Attorney <u>subject to discipline</u>?

A. Yes, because Attorney caused Engineer to leave the jurisdiction of the court for the purpose of making her unavailable as a witness.

B. Yes, because opposing counsel had not yet had a reasonable opportunity to learn of Engineer's views.

C. No, because Engineer's views were reduced to writing and are well known to many other employees of Corp.

D. No, unless there was a pending request for Engineer's testimony at the time the retirement offer was made to Engineer.

81.

Attorney represented Client in a personal injury action against the driver of the car in which Client was injured while a passenger. The personal injury action was settled, and Attorney received a check in the amount of $10,000 payable to Attorney. Attorney deposited the check in her Clients' Trust Account.

One day later, Attorney received a letter from Bank, which had heard of the settlement of the personal injury lawsuit. Bank informed Attorney that Client had failed to make his monthly mortgage payments for the last three months and demanded that Attorney immediately release $900 of the proceeds of the settlement to Bank or Bank would institute mortgage foreclosure proceedings against Client. Attorney informed Client of Bank's letter. Client responded:

> "I don't care what Bank does. The property is essentially worthless, so let Bank foreclose. If Bank wants to sue me, I'll be easy enough to find. I don't think they'll even bother. You just take your legal fees and turn the rest of the proceeds over to me."

Is Attorney <u>subject to discipline</u> if she follows Client's instructions?

A. Yes, if Client does not dispute the $900 debt to Bank.

B. Yes, because Attorney knew that Client was planning to force Bank to sue him.

C. No, unless Attorney had reason to believe that Client would not have sufficient funds to pay any subsequent judgment obtained by Bank.

D. No, because Bank has no established right to the specific proceeds of Client's personal injury judgment.

82.

Three lawyers, Alpha, Beta, and Delta, formed a partnership to practice law with offices in both State First and State Second. Alpha is admitted to practice only in State First. Beta is admitted to practice only in State Second, and Delta is admitted to practice in both States First and Second. The following letterhead is on stationery used by their offices in both states:

Alpha, Beta, and Delta

Attorneys at Law

100 State Street	200 Bank Building
City, State First	City, State Second
(200) 555-5555	(202) 555-5555

Attorney Alpha

Admitted to practice only

in State First

Attorney Beta

Admitted to practice only

in State Second

Attorney Delta

Admitted to practice

in States First and Second

Are the members of the partnership <u>subject to discipline</u>?

A. No, because the letterhead states the jurisdictions in which each partner is admitted.

B. Yes, because there is no jurisdiction in which both Alpha and Beta are admitted to practice.

C. Yes, because the firm name used by each office contains the name of a lawyer not admitted to practice in that jurisdiction.

D. Yes, unless Delta actively practices law in both States First and Second.

83.

Attorney was engaged under a general retainer agreement to represent Corp, a corporation involved in the uranium industry. Under the agreement, Attorney handled all of Corp's legal work, which typically involved regulatory issues and litigation.

Corp told Attorney that a congressional committee was holding hearings concerning the extent of regulation in the copper industry. Because Corp was considering buying a copper mine during the next fiscal year, Corp wanted Attorney to testify that the industry was overregulated. Attorney subsequently testified before the relevant congressional committee. Attorney registered his appearance under his own name and did not disclose that he was appearing on behalf of a client. Afterward, Attorney billed Corp for fees and expenses related to his testimony.

Was Attorney's conduct <u>proper</u>?

A. Yes, because the duty of confidentiality prevented Attorney from disclosing the identity of his client.

B. Yes, because the attorney-client evidentiary privilege prevented disclosure of the identity of his client in this context.

C. No, because Attorney failed to disclose that he was appearing and testifying in a representative capacity.

D. No, because Attorney accepted compensation in return for his testimony.

84.

Judge is one of three trustees of a trust for the educational benefit of her grandchildren. The trust owns 5,000 shares of stock in Big Oil Company. The stock has been selling for the past year at $10.00 per share. Big Oil is suing Oil Refining Company for breach of an oil refining agreement, and the case is assigned to Judge for trial. Judge believes that she can be fair and impartial.

<u>Must</u> Judge disqualify herself from the case?

A. Yes, because the trust has more than a de minimus financial interest in Big Oil Company.

B. Yes, unless the outcome of the lawsuit is unlikely to affect the value of the stock.

C. No, unless Judge personally owns stock in either party to the litigation.

D. No, because Judge believes she can remain impartial.

85.

For many years, Attorney has served as outside counsel to Corp, a corporation. Shortly after a change in management, Attorney discovered what she reasonably believed to be a material misstatement in a document she had drafted that Attorney was about to file on Corp's behalf with a government agency. Attorney advised Corp's Board of Directors that filing the document was probably criminal. However, the Board disagreed that there was any material misstatement and directed Attorney to proceed with the filing. When Attorney indicated her intention to resign, Corp argued that a resignation at this time would send a signal that there was a problem with the filing. Corp urged Attorney to continue the representation, but offered to use in-house counsel to complete the work on the filing. Although she does not know for certain that filing the document is illegal, Attorney reasonably believes that it is. In any event, Attorney is personally uncomfortable with the representation and wants to withdraw.

May Attorney withdraw from her representation of Corp?

A. Yes, because withdrawal is permitted but not required when a client insists on conduct which the lawyer reasonably believes, but does not know, will be criminal.

B. Yes, because withdrawal is required when a client insists on conduct which the lawyer reasonably believes, but does not know, will be criminal.

C. No, if Corp is correct that withdrawal would breach confidentiality by sending a signal that the filing is problematic.

D. No, if Attorney's withdrawal as outside counsel might affect Corp's ability to complete the filing in a timely fashion.

86.

Judge and Attorney were formerly law partners and during their partnership acquired several parcels of real property as co-tenants. After

Judge was elected to the trial court in County, she remained a co-tenant with Attorney, but left the management of the properties to Attorney.

Judge's term of office will expire soon and she is opposed for reelection by two members of the bar. Attorney, who has not discussed the matter with Judge, intends to make a substantial contribution to Judge's campaign for reelection.

Judge is one of fifteen judges sitting as trial court judges in County.

Is Attorney <u>subject to discipline</u> if Attorney contributes $10,000 to Judge's reelection campaign?

A. Yes, If Attorney frequently represents clients in cases tried in the trial court of County.

B. Yes, because Judge and Attorney have not discussed the matter of a campaign contribution.

C. No, if the contribution is made to a campaign committee organized to support Judge's reelection.

D. No, because Attorney and Judge have a long-standing personal and business relationship.

87.

Attorney Alpha, a partner in the law firm of Alpha & Beta, was retained by Plaint, the plaintiff in a personal injury action against Deft. The jury rendered a verdict in favor of Deft, and Alpha filed an appeal on Plaint's behalf. Alpha reviewed the trial transcript and wrote the brief. The brief stated, "It is uncontroverted that Deft failed to signal before turning left into the intersection." In fact, Wit, a witness called by Deft, testified that Deft did signal before turning. Alpha was aware of this testimony, having read it while reviewing the trial transcript.

Three days before the appeal was scheduled to be argued in the state's intermediate appellate court, Alpha suffered a heart attack. Attorney Beta, one of Alpha's partners, agreed to argue the appeal. Beta knew nothing about the case and had no opportunity to confer with Alpha. In preparing for the argument, Beta read Alpha's brief thoroughly and read as much of the trial transcript as was possible in the limited time available, but did not read Wit's testimony. In oral argument, Beta stated to the court, "Your honors, as stated in our brief, it is uncontroverted that Deft failed to signal before turning left into the intersection." Beta assumed that Alpha's statement in the brief to that effect was correct.

Is Beta <u>subject to discipline</u> for making this statement during oral argument?

A. Yes, because the statement was false.

B. Yes, because Beta did not know whether or not the statement was true.

C. No, because Beta did not know that the statement was false.

D. No, because all Beta did was to truthfully recount the statement made by Alpha in the brief.

88.

Judge needed to obtain a loan to be secured by a second mortgage on his house. Bank offered him a loan at a very favorable interest rate. The vice-president at Bank told Judge:

"Frankly, we normally don't give such a large loan when the security is a second mortgage, and your interest rate will be 2% less than we charge our other customers. But we know that your salary is inadequate, and we are giving you special consideration."

Is it <u>proper</u> for Judge to accept the loan?

A. Yes, if Judge does not act in any case involving Bank.

B. Yes, if Bank is not likely to be involved in litigation in the court on which Judge sits.

C. No, unless the same terms are available to all judges in the state.

D. No, because the amount of the loan and interest rate were not available to persons who were not judges.

89.

Law Firm has 300 lawyers in 10 states. It has placed the supervision of all routine administrative and financial matters in the hands of Admin, a nonlawyer. Admin is paid a regular monthly salary and a year-end bonus of 1% of Law Firm's net income from fees. Organizationally, Admin reports to Attorney, who is the managing partner of Law Firm. Attorney deals with all issues related to Law Firm's supervision of the practice of law.

Is it <u>proper</u> for Attorney to participate in Law Firm's use of Admin's services in this fashion?

A. Yes, unless Admin has access to client files.

B. Yes, if Admin does not control the professional judgment of the lawyers in the firm.

C. No, because Law Firm is sharing legal fees with a nonlawyer.

D. No, because Law Firm is assisting a nonlawyer in the unauthorized practice of law.

90.

Attorney experienced several instances when clients failed to pay their fees in a timely manner, but it was too late in the representation to withdraw without prejudicing the clients. To avoid a recurrence of this situation, Attorney has drafted a stipulation of consent to withdraw if fees are not paid according to the fee agreement. She proposes to have all clients sign the stipulation at the outset of the representation.

Is it <u>proper</u> for Attorney to use the stipulation to withdraw from representation whenever a client fails to pay fees?

A. Yes, because a lawyer may withdraw when the financial burden of continuing the representation would be substantially greater than the parties anticipated at the time of the fee agreement.

B. Yes, because the clients consented to the withdrawal in the stipulation.

C. No, because a client's failure to pay fees when due may be insufficient in itself to justify withdrawal.

D. No, unless clients are provided an opportunity to seek independent legal advice before signing the stipulation.

91.

Attorney was retained by Defendant to represent him in a paternity suit. Aunt, Defendant's aunt, believed the suit was unfounded and motivated by malice. Aunt sent Attorney a check for $1,000 and asked Attorney to apply it to the payment of Defendant's fee. Aunt told Attorney not to tell Defendant of the payment because "Defendant is too proud to accept gifts, but I know he really needs the money."

Is it <u>proper</u> for Attorney to accept Aunt's check?

A. Yes, if Aunt does not attempt to influence Attorney's conduct of the case.

B. Yes, if Attorney's charges to Defendant are reduced accordingly.

C. No, because Aunt is attempting to finance litigation to which she is not a party.

D. No, unless Attorney first informs Defendant and obtains Defendant's consent to retain the payment.

92.

Attorney has a highly efficient staff of paraprofessional legal assistants, all of whom are graduates of recognized legal assistant educational programs. Recently, the statute of limitations ran against a claim of a client of Attorney's when a legal assistant negligently misplaced Client's file and suit was not filed within the time permitted by law.

Which of the following correctly states Attorney's professional responsibility?

A. Attorney is <u>subject to civil liability</u> and is also <u>subject to discipline</u> on the theory of respondeat superior.

B. Attorney is <u>subject to civil liability</u> or is <u>subject to discipline</u> at Client's election.

C. Attorney is <u>subject to civil liability</u> but is NOT <u>subject to discipline</u> unless Attorney failed to supervise the legal assistant adequately.

D. Attorney is NOT <u>subject to civil liability</u> and is NOT <u>subject to discipline</u> if Attorney personally was not negligent.

93.

Attorney represented Plaint, who sued Deft for injuries Plaint sustained in a car accident. Prior to trial, Attorney interviewed Wit, who stated that she had observed Deft drinking heavily hours before the accident. Unfortunately, on the eve of trial, Wit informed Attorney that Wit was ill and could not testify at trial. Attorney tried but could not obtain a continuance. As a result, Plaint's direct case rested solely on Plaint's testimony that Deft was speeding and that Deft's car crossed the middle line and hit Plaint's car. Deft testified that he was driving safely in compliance with all rules and that the accident was entirely Plaint's fault. On cross-examination, Attorney asked Deft, "Isn't it a fact that you were drinking prior to the accident?" Deft answered that he had not consumed alcoholic beverages on the day of the accident. In summation to the jury, Attorney stated:

"Ladies and gentlemen of the jury, you and I know that Deft lied when he stated that he had not consumed alcoholic beverages on the day of the accident. We know that he was impaired."

On which of the following grounds, if any, is Attorney subject to discipline?

I. Attorney's question to Deft implying that Deft had consumed alcoholic beverages when Attorney knew that he could not offer evidence of Deft's drinking.

II. Attorney's statement to the jury asserting that Attorney knew that Deft was drunk when no evidence in the record supported this allegation

III. Attorney's statement asserting a personal belief that Deft was drunk and lying.

A. I and II, but not III

B. II and III, but not I

C. I, II, and III

D. Neither I, II, nor III

94.

Pros, a prosecutor, was assigned to try a criminal case against Deft, who was charged with robbery of a convenience store. Deft denied any involvement, contending he was home watching television with his mother on the night in question. At the trial, Wit, a customer at the convenience store, testified that he had identified Deft in a police line-up and provided other testimony connecting Deft to the crime. In addition, Pros entered into evidence a poor-quality videotape of the robbery as recorded by the store surveillance camera. The jury convicted Deft of the crime charged. Unknown to Deft's court-appointed lawyer, Wit had first identified another person in the police line-up and selected Deft only after encouragement by the detective. Pros was aware of these facts but did not notify Deft's counsel who made no pretrial discovery request to obtain this information.

Is Pros subject to discipline?

A. Yes, unless the jury could make its own identification of Deft from the videotape.

B. Yes, because this information tended to negate Deft's guilt.

C. No, because Deft's counsel made no pretrial discovery request to obtain this information.

D. No, unless it is likely that the jury would have acquitted Deft had it known that Wit first identified someone else.

95.

Attorney and Client entered into a written retainer and hourly fee agreement that required Client to pay $5,000 in advance of any services rendered by Attorney and which required Attorney to return any portion of the $5,000 that was not earned. The agreement further provided that Attorney would render monthly statements and withdraw her fees as billed. The agreement was silent as to whether the $5,000 advance was to be deposited in Attorney's Clients' Trust Account or in a general account. Attorney deposited the entire fund in her Clients' Trust Account, which also contained the funds of other persons which had been entrusted to Attorney. Thereafter, Attorney rendered monthly progress reports and statements for services to Client after services were rendered, showing the balance of Client's fee advance. However, Attorney did not withdraw any of the $5,000 advance until one year later when the matter was concluded to Client's complete satisfaction. At that time, Attorney had billed Client reasonable legal fees of $4,500. Attorney wrote two checks on her Clients' Trust Account: one to herself for $4,500, which she deposited in her general office account, and one for $500 to Client.

Was Attorney's conduct <u>proper</u>?

A. Yes, because Attorney deposited the funds in her Clients' Trust Account.

B. Yes, because Attorney rendered periodic and accurate billings.

C. No, because Attorney's failure to withdraw her fees as billed resulted in an impermissible commingling of her funds and Clients' funds.

D. No, because Attorney required an advanced payment against her fee.

96.

Attorneys Alpha and Beta had been political opponents. Alpha was elected to the state legislature after a bitter race in which Beta had managed the campaign of Alpha's opponent. Alpha had publicly blamed Beta at that time for what Alpha reasonably believed were illegal and unethical campaign practices and later had publicly objected to Beta's appointment as a judge.

Alpha represented Client in a widely publicized case tried in Judge Beta's court. At the conclusion of the trial, Beta ruled against Alpha's client. Alpha then held a press conference and said "All that you reporters have to do is check your files and you will know what I think about Judge Beta's character and fitness."

Is Alpha subject to discipline for making this statement?

A. Yes, if Alpha's statement might lessen confidence in the legal system

B. Yes, because Alpha's past accusations were unrelated to Beta's legal knowledge.

C. No, because Alpha reasonably believed that the statements about Beta were true.

D. No, if Beta had equal access to the press.

97.

Judge, a judge in a criminal trial court of State, wishes to serve as guardian of her father, who has been declared incompetent. Accepting the responsibilities of the position would not interfere with the performance of Judge's official duties. Although the position in all likelihood would not involve contested litigation, it would be necessary for Judge to prepare and sign various pleadings, motions, and other papers and to appear in civil court on her father's behalf.

Would it be proper for Judge to undertake this guardianship?

A. Yes, unless Judge receives compensation for her services as guardian.

B. Yes, because the position involves a close family member and will not interfere with Judge's performance of her judicial duties.

C. No, because the position will require Judge to appear in court.

D. No, because the position will require Judge to prepare and sign pleadings, motions, and other papers.

98.

Client hired Attorney Alpha to file a lawsuit against Client's former employer, Corp, for wrongful discharge. Alpha filed the suit in federal district court based upon three grounds. It turned out that a unanimous

US Supreme Court decision had recently eliminated the third ground as a theory available to plaintiffs in wrongful discharge cases. Attorney Beta, who represents Corp, filed a motion alleging that the complaint was based upon a theory (the third ground) that is no longer supported by existing law and cited the new decision. Within ten days after the filing of the complaint, Alpha withdrew the third ground and continued with the litigation.

Is Alpha subject to litigation sanction?

A. Yes, unless Alpha discussed the adverse legal authority with Client before filing the complaint.

B. Yes, because Alpha should have cited the US Supreme Court decision in the complaint.

C. No, because Alpha withdrew the third ground within ten days after filing the complaint.

D. No, unless Alpha knew or should have known of the recent decision when the complaint was filed.

Answer Key to Sample Questions

1.	C	26.	A	51.	C	76.	D
2.	B	27.	B	52.	D	77.	B
3.	B	28.	A	53.	C	78.	B
4.	C	29.	B	54.	D	79.	C
5.	C	30.	A	55.	A	80.	A
6.	D	31.	C	56.	C	81.	D
7.	D	32.	B	57.	D	82.	A
8.	A	33.	A	58.	B	83.	C
9.	A	34.	D	59.	B	84.	A
10.	C	35.	B	60.	D	85.	A
11.	D	36.	C	61.	B	86.	C
12.	A	37.	B	62.	C	87.	C
13.	D	38.	D	63.	B	88.	D
14.	C	39.	D	64.	B	89.	B
15.	A	40.	B	65.	D	90.	C
16.	D	41.	C	66.	D	91.	D
17.	A	42.	B	67.	A	92.	C
18.	D	43.	D	68.	B	93.	B
19.	B	44.	B	69.	A	94.	B
20.	D	45.	A	70.	A	95.	C
21.	C	46.	C	71.	B	96.	C
22.	A	47.	A	72.	B	97.	B
23.	C	48.	C	73.	D	98.	C
24.	B	49.	B	74.	C		
25.	A	50.	C	75.	B